Jesus
Meet
Me

Knowing A Personal God

MEAGAN & REBECCA
AHLSTROM

ISBN: 978-0-9714147-2-3
Published by Point to Point LLC
Nashville, Tennessee

Cover Design - Robyn Martins
Editor - Kathryn Ritcheske
Consultant - Melody (Ahlstrom) Harmon
Graphics Consultant - Kyrstin Avello

Scripture references are from the NIV unless otherwise noted.

Dedication

To Olive, Finley and Kingston and those yet to come who were not given the opportunity to know Meagan. What a treasure to have her heart within the pages of this book. I hope as you grow, you are inspired by your Aunt Meagan's writings and allow yourself to experience the passion for Christ she had. He will meet you; you need but to ask.

Table of Contents

Acknowledgements

To my husband and soul-mate Leo, I am beyond blessed. You have been my strong shoulder even in your own pain and continue to be an example of unwavering faith. After 30+ years, I am still captivated by your heart!

Melody, our youngest and a young mother herself, you have such a tender heart and yet a tenacious faith. You have been such a help with this project—quick to protect your older sister Meagan and that warms *this* mother's soul. You have been a strong voice on this journey and my song in the night.

To my Meagan, I miss you! I long for the day that I see you again and worship our Lord together from *your* view! Thank you for sharing the passion of journaling and leaving us such treasures. "I carry your heart with me (I carry it in my heart)" [tu Misma]

Aaron, our oldest, you have been a source of gentle strength and spiritual truths since you were a boy. You are a steady ship when the oceans of life overwhelm me. Even when your own life is much to bear, you are always a safe place for me to rest.

To my parents, Caro and Shirleen Louviere, thank you for always being present and such a strong presence, balancing the truths that encourage and the truths that sting. Thank you for planting the seeds for my faith. I love you to the moon! And to the rest of my wonderful family, I thank God for you as we walk this journey called "Life."

I especially thank all of our friends in the Chicago-burbs, Tennessee, throughout the United States and across the oceans, for being the hands and feet of Christ to me and my family. My heart overflows.

Lastly, I acknowledge the ONE who stands high above the rest—my Sovereign Lord. You never let go!!

Job 1:21

"The Lord gave and the Lord has taken away;
   may the name of the Lord be praised."

Introduction

Rebecca L. Ahlstrom

Every time I doubt the presence of God on this journey, a voice in the depths of my soul reminds me that I would have perished had it not been for His grace. Though the darkness often clouds my vision, He has been with me in the greatest way—He never let go of me! He has been relentless to fight for me; strong in my weakness; and even grieves with me. God has been at work, and His fingerprints along the way are most evident. It is by His mercy that the waves of despair have not destroyed me; the fires of guilt have not consumed me; the weight of grief has not crushed me. I recall the old hymn, "Great is Thy faithfulness! Morning by morning new mercies I see; all I have needed Thy hand hath provided; Great is Thy faithfulness, Lord unto me!" He never let go!

Our family and friends suffered a great loss the morning of June 14, 2009. Not just the loss of someone dearly loved, but the loss of a great and mighty light—a light that didn't ask permission to shine.

My daughter Meagan (24) and I were returning from a road trip and only an hour from home when a drunk driver, who passed out at the wheel, crashed into our car. Meagan, driving at the time, turned the wheel and took the brunt of the hit. Her life ended upon impact. I sustained injuries, but it was my faith that suffered the hardest blow as I now find my life thrust into a journey of trials unthinkable. This journey has rendered me on a spiritual quest to rediscover a God I thought I knew.

Bearing the weight of grief and utter shock, I held fast to my faith, the Bible, and Meagan's journals. Meagan and I are avid journalers, as are my two other children. Out of an indescribable longing, I opened her journal to one of her last entries and was captivated. I kept reading and was brought to my knees. My husband Leo (Meagan's dad) and I were humbled by the depth of her writings and recognized we were given a gift, a treasure, something most parents don't have—our daughter Meagan left behind journals filled with penned conversations. Some about life, some about love, most are directed to the One she adored—her Savior, her Lord.

It is through Meagan's journal entries that I began to find purpose and my heart began to turn. I have God's Word and her word daily keeping me alive. She was a life coach for me since she was a teenager, and now her writings are an encouragement in the darkest of times—Jesus meets me in the abyss of despair and draws me out often with Meagan's written words.

A few months after June 2009, I felt compelled to share her writings. If Meagan's journal entries could speak life to my aching heart, then I had to let her passion inspire family and friends. I could no longer keep her journals to myself. So I began posting one entry at a time on social media outlets. Through the journey, her writings and God's revelations have prompted writings of my own that I have shared. And the responses have been overwhelming!

Jesus Meet Me is a collaborative work of mother and daughter: writings of Meagan's that inspire the soul and challenge one's thinking; along with writings of mine in response to a shaken faith, an ever-aching heart, a soul learning to trust again, and a life experiencing the fingerprints of God in all the details.

Through Meagan's journal entries, I pray that you will see evidence of a life well lived amidst the struggles of life itself. I believe that you will witness a passionate relationship between Meagan and her Creator...how it can be...how it should be.

It is my hope that my writings (in italics throughout the book to distinguish from Meagan's journal entries) will reflect a God who remains ever-present through the darkness, steady through the storms, and infinitely patient through the healing. It is also my hope that you will be captivated by this collection of writings and find your own heart passionately pursuing a personal Lord.

Micah 7:8b

Though I have fallen, I will rise.

Though I sit in darkness,
   the Lord will be my light.

I Will Meet You

Meagan E. Ahlstrom

[This is Meagan's journal entry that I read at her memorial service. It gave insight to her very soul, and as I said that night, it is everything I could ever want to know. This is "our Meagan" days before the tragedy.]

I never once gave myself any room to get to know "me." To find any confidence in who I am. I came closer to that point my last year in Nashville, but I didn't quite step into it until recently.

Maybe I'm just older and wiser. Maybe it was about being in a different place and discovering something new. But whatever did it, I feel I am so very much in the right place. I feel...like I'm my own person. Lord, I've waited my whole life to feel this way! What an amazing feeling! It has taken me so long to get here, and yet, I am only 24. What a blessing!

Lord, thank You for sparing my life and allowing me to live a life so different than the one I was choosing for myself.

You are such an incredible God. I deserve nothing, and yet You choose to bless me daily. Thank You, Jesus. I miss You. I love You. I will meet You.

My Author

Meagan E. Ahlstrom

My life is a play.
Some days I star in it;
Other days I walk through, a mere extra.
Only I have the script.
Few people hear what it contains.
Those who don't hear it hate it.
Those who do hear it question it.
However, some neither question nor hate.
They simply watch and are a good audience.
A choice few in this audience can direct,
And often do I look for their direction.
But there's only One who truly gives me guidance.
One who always supports me,
Never criticizing, only helping and loving.
This One is the Author.
The Author of my script.
The Author of all scripts.
The Author of Life.

Shall We Meet Again Tomorrow?

Meagan E. Ahlstrom

Throughout my day at work rarely do we talk about life or death or life after death. And not that everything has to be so heavy, but if I truly without a doubt believe there is a living God and a heaven and a hell, and that those who do not recognize Christ as their Lord and Savior may suffer in hell, shouldn't I voice my concern to those around me whom I meet, whom I care about? Shouldn't I warn them if I love them, if I have even the slightest feelings for them at all? Shouldn't I, if I am a Christian? What is there that is more important to talk about than that? What if that is the sole purpose of me moving here and having this job? What if I am missing everyday an opportunity for God to use me? Then...what am I doing?

Thank You, God, for speaking to me in such a clear way. How funny, really. All I did was pick up a book to spend a little time with You, and BAM! You were right there waiting.

Thank You for that. Shall we meet again tomorrow? Yes, of course! Tomorrow!

Dear God

Meagan E. Ahlstrom

Do I ever take You for granted?
Do I say "I love you" enough?
You have given me life and forgiveness,
And to top it all—You give me love.

Knowing who I am, and who I was,
And that You never turned me away,
Brings tears to my eyes in gratefulness,
Yet I wonder have I said "thank you" today?

Yes, in habit, and some in knowing,
But have I ever fallen to my knees,
And humbled myself long enough to pray,
"I'm sorry, Father, forgive me"?

Heartfelt, spirit-spoken, and sincere,
Have I cried just to be near?
Have I shared my heart and the things I know
You know but still want to hear?

It's hard for me, it really is,
To know all the days I shall live,
Can never reflect the depth of my love for you—
But my life is all I have to give.

I know I ask for so many things,
But please have mercy when I fail.
Hold my hand and lift me up again,
So in those times I will prevail.

And if You ever need anything—ever I am Yours,
I am a vessel ready to do Your will.
I make a vow to You for the rest of my life:
I repent! I will be different! I will!

Totally Out of Control

Meagan E. Ahlstrom

I think I'm beginning to realize just how important it is to seek God DAILY and surround oneself with people who do the same. My whole attitude, the way I feel, even my outlook on life have all changed drastically.

I have been spending more time in the Word. I have been praying more. Therapy, of course, has been a great tool, and since my counselor is a Christian there are some sessions that feel more like Bible studies than actual sessions—which is great.

Most importantly, I've decided to change. I gave up trying to have control over every situation, and I have laid all my burdens at the feet of the Lord. God has been so good and so faithful. He is giving me such peace and comfort in this time, and it is amazing how quickly He is answering my prayers now that I am truly seeking His face and His will.

It's as if everything in my life is starting to reflect the goodness of God. And I am so hungry. And I am so happy. There are still problems I must face all around me, but I am happy.

I am beginning to feel more complete. I am beginning to feel more complete in "me" and more complete in the Lord. What a great feeling! I feel 20 pounds lighter. I can't stop smiling. I feel so loved. I know God is with me, holding my hand, and now GLADLY taking care of my mess since I have finally laid it all at His feet.

I can honestly say right now that I have no worries—not one! I am so happy! I am so excited about where I am! I am so excited about where I am going!

WHO WOULD HAVE EVER THOUGHT THAT BEING TOTALLY OUT OF CONTROL WOULD FEEL SO WONDERFUL!

1 Timothy 3:13

Those who have served well gain an excellent standing and great assurance in their faith in Christ Jesus.

You Cry

Rebecca L. Ahlstrom

It was a tough day. I could not see past my deep sorrow of losing my Meagan. I even leaned outside and yelled to the birds, "How can you be singing?!" The quiet of our home became filled with the groaning of my soul in utter despair. I curled up on the floor, pleading with God to take my life.

I am honest with the Lord when I am alone with Him. My conversations are raw and very candid, though never disrespectful. Sometimes "knowing" the Word can be just as dangerous as "not knowing" it. One of the hardest facts for me to process and accept is that all things go through the hands of God, as in Romans 11:36: "For from him and through him and for him are all things...." And though He could have prevented the death of my daughter, He chose not to.

Today was one of those days that my heart was screaming in agony. I miss my daughter. I miss her laughter. I miss her drama. I miss our deep conversations about real life issues. I miss our silly conversations and tickle fights. I miss her calling me "Misma." I miss her life-coaching that challenged me spiritually. I miss sharing with her my faith that inspired her to dig deeper. I miss it all! And today I needed to talk to her. Today He needed to let me talk to her!

I cried. I cried to my Father for mercy. The mother's heart within me could not be comforted as I groaned for my daughter's hug. My conscience pleaded for mercy because I was so close to the cliff of insanity—a terrifying feeling.

Then I heard Him. From the pit of darkness, I heard that oh so familiar voice. It was strong. It was sovereign. It was overwhelming. It was piercing. "You cry as though she is yours."

My soul was quieted by a cradled chastisement from my Lord. The tears stopped. Dumbfounded by the simple choice of words, I reflected on the fact that Meagan had given her life to the Lord as a young girl, and her writings, the ones I have come to cherish, are filled with passionate letters to the One she adored. She is no longer mine. I was her caretaker. I was her closest friend. I was her buddy. But she is no longer mine. And my tears transposed into humble prayers of repentance.

I'm sorry, Lord. Why do I question You so often? I don't understand any of this, and I constantly struggle with all the "whys" even though I know You have spared Meagan from so much. Forgive me. I give You my heart in all of its humanness. I'm trying to give You me.

Psalm 116:7

Return to your rest, my soul,
for the Lord has been good to you.

Revelation

Meagan E. Ahlstrom

I have always been extremely good at wearing my heart WAY out on my sleeve. And it hasn't always served me well. In fact, MANY times it hasn't served me well.

It took me moving and really letting go, truly offering my desires up to the Lord, laying things down and moving on, and getting out of His way for change to happen. It took getting out of my own way so that God could get to "me"!

You know, when I first moved here [to the Chicago-suburbs], I could almost feel Him say that He's missed me. It breaks my heart to think of how careless I was with my relationship with Him.

Now, above all else, I will honor God—with my life, with my actions, with my heart. Go figure, once I get that right, things become better!

The Only Ones Worth Having Anyway

Meagan E. Ahlstrom

I'm really in the mood to write right now. About what? I have no idea—but I am too tired to do so. Thus is my life nowadays—constantly tired with no time to do the things I really want. I guess that's not true. I have some time. I'm just so exhausted I can never really concentrate to do anything worthwhile with it. Even now, I feel like I am making absolutely no sense.

I think I exhaust myself in a lot of ways—separate from the normal, daily obligations that cause one to be tired. I believe my mind is always going crazy with thoughts of how I want things to be. I can never just enjoy the moment and where I am. I never want to stay in the same place for too long. I wear myself out always thinking I should be somewhere else, doing other things. Thinking I will never have enough time; that I am running out of time. When in reality, all these crazy thoughts, this bogged-down mentality is causing me to be confused, overwhelmed, and unproductive. I get less done thinking I should be doing more than if I would just concentrate on what is in front of me and giving it my best so that other opportunities will follow.

I am just such a big dreamer, and that's exciting…sure. But it's also very dangerous.

I really want to start working on that. Staying in one spot. Being still. Waiting for the right opportunity. Finishing what I start. Honoring my commitments. Trusting God.

I feel I have missed out on so many God opportunities because I can't stop thinking about my agenda. But the truth is, my agenda is getting me nowhere. Truth is, I only want the God opportunities. They are the only ones worth having anyway.

Okay, it's bedtime.

This Mediocre Life

Meagan E. Ahlstrom

I don't pray enough. I don't study enough. I don't read the Word enough. I am in a slump. There! I admitted it…to myself. Finally.

Here I am, praying for Your best, yet I don't put myself in a posture to achieve that "best." I am not saying it is by "works," but how can I expect Your best, Lord, when I don't spend quality time with You? When I don't even open myself up to Your best?

Wow! I need some serious help. I am so tired of living this mediocre life. I don't want to be angry anymore. I don't want to be negative. I don't want to be so toxic. Help me. Forgive me. And convict me every second. Please, Lord. I want to live better. Live right. There is no point in living at all if it's not with You.

Please, clean out my heart. I will do my part. I vow to pray, to read, to seek You again wholeheartedly. Please meet me. Purify my heart. Strengthen my spirit, Lord. Show me how to live a life for You again. Please, Father.

Amen! Amen! Amen!

The Only Eyes that Matter

Meagan E. Ahlstrom

The truth is—a sin is a sin is a sin. No sin holds any more weight in the eyes of the Lord than any other. God knows we all sin, and your sins will NOT condemn you to a life any less than that of what the Lord has for you. When you sincerely ask for forgiveness, you are forgiven. Maybe not in the eyes of the world, maybe not in the eyes of man, but surely in the eyes of the Lord—the ONLY eyes that matter. In the eyes of anyone else I will always fall short, I will always fail, I will look weak. But to My Lord, I am something so priceless that He had to give Himself, sacrifice His life, just so He could spend eternity with me! If that is not something to feel incredible about, I do not know what is!

Children will disappoint their parents. They will disobey them and may not turn to them in all issues. Therefore, my children will know NO sin is greater than my love for them. NO sin will matter more to me than their life or their love, and no sin will deny them the greatness they deserve. Seek His face, ask for forgiveness, live a life striving to be in His will, and all good things WILL come your way. In due time, all good things!

1 John 3:1

See what great love the Father has lavished on us, that we should be called children of God! And that is what we are!

"God, It's Me. It's Meagan."

Rebecca L. Ahlstrom

Part of the impact Meagan had in this life was her impact on me. Although there are many examples, I want to share one story of how her faith challenged me in a way that changed me forever.

Meagan was in high school when she became sick with a serious stomach virus. It was a terrible virus, probably the worst I have ever seen. It hit her hard in the early evening and lasted the WHOLE night long. The waves of violent sickness (throwing up) came frequently and without mercy. Each time, I would gently put a cold washcloth on her face, stroke her hair, and pray earnestly for God's healing. We repeated this over and over and over…hour after hour after torturous hour.

We had a bay window in our bathroom where I made her a comfy resting place for the few minutes in between surges. It broke my heart as a mom to see her in such agony and know I could do nothing to help. The bay window was not an option for long before she ended up curled on the hard floor and pleaded not to be "adjusted." After hours of sitting with her, I decided to lie on my bed—even if it was for only minutes at a time. When the next wave hit, I would run in as before. By now, it was early morning. I heard her stirring again and thought surely this has to end soon. She is exhausted. Her body can't go anymore. Lord, you have to end this! But no…

As I ran toward her, I heard her talking to God while hugging the toilet. I stopped and didn't go further. Her conversation was different from those hours before. This was personal…really personal. Her voice was soft and endearing. Her next words brought me literally to my knees. She said, "God, it's me. It's Meagan." Something happened to me at that moment. I was awakened to the fact that my daughter, my Meagan, had a relationship with her Father that I didn't have. I had been a Christ-follower for at least twenty years at this point, and never have I ever approached God like Meagan did—with such humble confidence, such assurance. She knew her Father. And she was confident He knew her—and by name.

That morning began my new pursuit—to have the assurance and faith that my daughter had. It took a while to rid myself of some bad thinking and open my eyes to Christ's mercy and grace, but I finally got there.

(Making a hard right turn to present day...)

June 14th shattered me. To be talking and singing in the car one moment and then witness my daughter killed 12 inches beside me the next, in the very seat I was just in, has tested every inch of my faith. The many "whys" of that night seem to scream louder than the "who" is in control. I have come to know a pain that I never knew existed and a longing that cannot be quenched. It is a constant struggle to keep darkness at a distance and choose to rest in God's grace.

And although I temporarily lost my "assurance" over the last few years, He never let go of me! I can once again pray with sweet confidence like Meagan, "God, it's me. It's Rebecca."

John 10:27-30

My sheep listen to My voice; I know them, and they follow Me. I give them eternal life, and they shall never perish; no one will snatch them out of My hand. My Father, who has given them to Me, is greater than all; no one can snatch them out of My Father's hand. I and the Father are one.

It's Time

Meagan E. Ahlstrom

[Meagan felt compelled to leave Nashville and move to where her father and I had relocated in the Chicago area. She said God was relentlessly tugging at her heart saying, "It's time." Within a few months, she made the move in faith and lived there with us for her last nine months.]

Lord, what gift have You placed in me? What is my mission here? I know it is to be Your light and tell people about You, but how, Lord? How am I going to do that? With what tool? In what way?

Maybe this move to Chicago will reveal more of Your plan for me. Maybe I should stop wondering and just continue being obedient. Lord, I want to be ready for You...for all You have for me...for my future...for what I am supposed to do.

Whatever life I live, whatever You have for me, will be nothing without You. I only want to live a life that You have Your hand on. An extraordinary life that could never have been accomplished without the favor and grace of God. A life that will reach millions. A life that will make a difference.

Grace and favor, Father, please. Keep Your hand on me. Show me what I need to see in Chicago. Show me where to go...with school...with work...with everything. I want to move when You say "move." I want to go where You want me. I want to live a life that people cannot understand. A life that reflects something supernatural. A life that makes people believe and see something outside of themselves. A life filled with Your grace and Your favor. Please, Father. I will work hard. I will be obedient.

Show me where to go. Show me what to do. Show me why You said, "It's time."

Keep Your hand on me, please. I love You, Father. I love You. I am ready.

Set Time

Meagan E. Ahlstrom

My dreams are so close,
I can almost taste it!

Everything I've longed for
Is just a breath away.

I have wanted this forever.
I know I can make it!

This is the time—the year—the day!

A Great New Place!

Meagan E. Ahlstrom

New place…

New chapter in my life…

But an entirely different person.

And here is why I love to write. Though looking back and rereading entries may be hard or at times even embarrassing, how amazing it is to see how far you've come. To see where life has taken you. To see how you've changed. To see "you." To really see you become the person you hope to be. The person you want to be or just the person you are meant to be. What a remarkable thing. And what a great new place!

Thank You, Jesus.

James 1:12

Blessed is the one who perseveres under trial because, having stood the test, that person will receive the crown of life that the Lord has promised to those who love Him.

Everything You Want, Lord

Rebecca L. Ahlstrom

For years on and off while our children were growing up and Leo was on the road with NewSong, a contemporary Christian band, I was in a season of deep pursuit of God and also deep surrender. In the midnight hours when all was quiet inside and out, I would make my way to the middle of our large backyard, stand with outstretched arms, look up to the velvet black skies, and cry out to God of the Universe, "Whatever You want, Lord! Whatever You want!" I would stand there blanketed in the blackness of the night for what seemed like hours—aware only of the glorious silence of His Presence.

One night stands out from all the rest. My children sleeping. Leo traveling. I again stood outside, looked up to the heavens, and called out the same prayer as I had so many times before, "Whatever You want, Lord! Whatever You want!" Yet, this time I heard something back. A voice. A voice that pierced my soul. Not an audible voice, but that kind of voice that shakes you deep within your spirit so that you know that you know that you know...it was real. And it was God. That kind of voice that changes you forever though none may understand or believe. This voice spoke to my soul a statement of complete surrender, "Not 'whatever' You want, but 'EVERYTHING' You want." Could this be a holy correction from my Creator Himself? My arms fell and I dropped to my knees. HE heard me! And He answered!

From that day forward when I was compelled outside into the night, my cry with outstretched arms was as He directed, "Everything You want, Lord! Everything You want!" And I would stand there in surrender.

I continued this until June 14th, when life and death intersected right before my eyes. And every part of my being was shattered. Every part of my faith was being tested. I never spoke of this, but there I was in wreckage meant to destroy me. My daughter sacrificed her life for mine. Her spirit ushered into Glory. And I—I was left in such utter darkness in the barren fields that I did not even see her on the floor of the car by my side for at least a minute. The darkness that used to awaken my soul had now become my worst nightmare. I was alone. And in that moment for just a second, I remembered my cry of so many nights, "Everything…" But I became quickly engulfed in the indescribable, unbearable, horrendous, agonizing pain of my great loss—the loss of my Meagan and the loss of "me" as I knew her.

I've been on a difficult journey once again in desperate pursuit of God. But this time, I'm discovering the God HE wants me to know. He has taken me to the ocean depths and through ruthless wilderness so that I would discover more of Him and His Greatness. I have discovered that He would no longer live in the "God box" I created for Him. He has busted the box wide open and has taken me to new places. He is creating a "new me" out of the wreckage.

*Leo and I were on a mission's trip in the Czech Republic for ten days recently—at a camp for 20-year-olds. I pursued God frantically every morning with the dawn. Near the end of our trip during our team meeting, I shared that God faithfully woke me up EVERY morning between 4:30 and 5:20. I would quickly get dressed, put on Meagan's pink Puma sneakers, grab my journals, and take off for long hikes on the very narrow roads of the mountains…in pursuit. It wasn't until one of the last days that I had an awakening: maybe God wasn't waking me up every morning before everyone else because He KNOWS how much I need my quiet time with Him to "process" my life and "accept" my hard reality. Maybe—He was waking me up because **HE** wanted to be with **ME**. (Even now I can't help but cry at the thought.)*

With this awakening, I picked up a rock on the path as I have the whole trip symbolic of my encounters with God. (God's people in the

Old Testament, when they experienced God or His deliverance, etc., would gather rocks and build an altar and then name it accordingly.) My rocks made it through U.S. Customs and are placed in our sunroom, each from a different place, each representing a different meaning. Yesterday, as I was journaling about this experience and my rocks, I felt an urgency to "name" them. Without pause, I was prompted the first one was to be called "The Place of My Knowing."

Though I have not cried out, "Everything You want, Lord!" since the tragedy, He doesn't seem to mind. In fact, He knows my heart and is obviously walking this journey with me—many times carrying me. I will get there. I NEVER turned my back on Him because HE is My Savior, My Redeemer, My Deliverer. He WILL see me to my deliverance where I can once again cry aloud with outstretched arms, "EVERYTHING, LORD. EVERYTHING!"

Psalm 141:1-2

I call to You, Lord; come quickly to me,
  hear me when I call to You.

May my prayer be set before You like incense;
  may the lifting up of my hands be like the evening
  sacrifice.

Maybe

Meagan E. Ahlstrom

My heart is in so many different places…. Torn between what I feel I *should* do and what I wish I *could* do…. The constant conflict between responsibility and desire. Fear and ambition. One always pressing to win. Me being the one who always loses.

Between my head and my heart, I would suffer a terrible life of confusion and frustration if not for God. Though I do at times feel moments of confusion or frustration or disappointment, it is more due to my inability to completely "let go and let God" than it is the lack of His presence and offering of peace.

Some days I feel I should just totally let go…and live a simple life, serving the Lord. Other days I think my heart is too big and my head is too full. I believe in the impossible. I think surely God gave me these feelings, this drive, these extraordinary dreams for a purpose. But where's the balance? The balance would have to be from God.

Moving to Chicago was supposed to be the next big step. Granted, I moved because I was being obedient to what I know I heard from the Lord, and maybe that *was* the step. Maybe *that* was the whole point. God asked me to move to see how much I trusted Him, to see if I would listen. And looking at it, it was a big step. But now that I'm here, all I can think about is, "What's next?"

I wonder where I'll be in life when I begin to feel a level of satisfaction. If I'll ever feel contentment. How old will I be? Where will I live? What will I be doing?

What's strange is if I were to die today, I'd be okay. I wouldn't have any huge regrets. Heaven will be so much better than anything here on earth.

The only thing that will matter is that I lived a life loving the Lord and my family and those close to me. And I know I've done that. I'm not a perfect person, but I know that the people in my life know I love them. And I am certain I have loved with my whole heart, which makes me think— maybe that's it. Maybe that's what it is all about. Maybe I already have it all worked out.

Maybe.

And That's All I Need to Know

Meagan E. Ahlstrom

I would like to be strong enough that I can be still...quiet...alone...with no noise, no TV, no music, no phone...and not worry! What is so wrong with just being by myself? And what is it in me that desperately needs phone calls or texts or attention? Not attention, really, as much as just the feeling of being needed. Wanted. Lord, fill that void in me. I don't want these insecurities. Show me I need no one but You.

Show me how to be strong. And strengthen the things in me that are growing. Help me see that I am complete in You, Lord. And that there is truly nothing else I need.

I am a Christian. I have Your love and Christ in my heart. You will never leave me. And that is all I need to know.

I love You. Amen.

The Will of the Lord Will Meet Me

Meagan E. Ahlstrom

I keep thinking about when my friend Luis and I went to Oak Park [a Chicago suburb] a few months ago. We went to the Ernest Hemingway Museum, and I saw an exhibit that showed young Ernest as a schoolboy.

When he was about 16, I believe, he was given an assignment to write about what he wanted to be/do when he grew up. He wrote, "I want to travel and write."

I stood at that particular spot in the museum, gazing up at those words for I don't know how long. Luis eventually had to find me and ask if I was ready to move on. I pointed out what I had seen, but he didn't seem near as fascinated as I was...as I still am.

I have always held a very serious admiration for those people who can sum up their life's ambition in one sentence...in one word. For me, I want...so many things.

Sometimes I do wish I could sum up every dream of mine in a simple sentence. Sometimes I wish I was really good at only one thing instead of being pretty good at a few. Then I see how silly it is to wish for something that I do not have...something that I am not.

And although I can't do things like others, that doesn't mean I can't do great things. In fact, the fact that I cannot put all of my energy in to one goal might actually make me great at many things. It just might take me a little longer to get there.

One thing is for certain: I refuse to allow anyone around me to say I am not "passionate" about anything simply because that person believes in the one-word-goal tactic.

The fact that I have many desires, I feel, makes me not necessarily a more passionate person, but a more well-rounded passionate person. In a way, I feel I can balance passion in many areas of life instead of just one.

I feel deeply for a great many things, and when I "grow up," I want…a great many things!

I know God has a very specific call for my life. And though I may not see it in its entirety now, He does…and that's all that matters.

I will continue to grow. I will continue to study. I will continue to follow, and I will continue to seek. And I am certain the will of the Lord will meet me, and I will be exactly where I need to be.

Romans 12:2

Do not conform to the pattern of this world, but be transformed by the renewing of your mind. Then you will be able to test and approve what God's will is—His good, pleasing and perfect will.

Speechless

Rebecca L. Ahlstrom

Lord, be near! Be near!

I'm placing myself on Your workbench this morning, Father. It's very early, just You and me. Do what only You can do. Do Your work on my heart, Lord. I am so desperate.

Be near, O God! Help me today. I so miss my Meagan! How can I focus on anything when my heart is screaming so loudly? Help.

"Let the mourning bring me word of your unfailing love." Wow! I've quoted this scripture (Psalm 143:8) for years, and I just misspelled "morning." Proof my heart is in pain. Proof...I need my Father.

Quiet. Still. Pause.

A melody came to mind that is stuck in my head:

> *It's my desire*
> *To look at you and smile*
> *To know the things you are*
> *And know you love me*

Stuck in my mind, over and over, I sing it...to You.

Wow, You are doing a work in the depths of my aching soul! Phew...tears! Keep me. Hold me in the palms of Your sovereign hands.

I called Leo and mentioned this chorus that won't leave me—a chorus I keep singing under my breath—but then I began to cry when I realize how those words fell out from my lips, through my pen, into my soul.

But a revelation came to me. Maybe, just maybe, it wasn't me singing to You. Maybe it was You and Your thoughts toward me!

Broken. Speechless. Held.

Psalm 123:1-2

I lift up my eyes to You,
   to You who sit enthroned in heaven.

As the eyes of slaves look to the hand of their master,
   as the eyes of a female slave look to the hand of her
   mistress,
so our eyes look to the Lord our God,
   till He shows us His mercy.

"Meagan"

Meagan E. Ahlstrom

I prefer tea to coffee. I would much rather stay up late than wake up early. I could spend all day in a bookstore, never even making a purchase, and be totally happy. My absolute favorite movies are French films. I don't even have to know what it is about or who is in it. Just tell me it's a French film and it will fast become my favorite! *Toi et Moi*, *Paris, Je T'Aime*, *Molière*! I love them all!

New pens and notebooks and sheets of blank paper excite me to no end! Even if I don't use them; even if I write nothing at all, just knowing I have them when I am ready is exciting.

I love watching TV shows or movies that have anything to do with New York City in the spring or fall or that have main characters who are writers. I absolutely despise doing anything social unless somehow it's educational. I would hate to get all dressed up and go downtown unless it was to see a new exhibit, art gallery, or museum. Then, not only would I go, I would be excited!

My idea of a great weekend away is to stay at a great hotel downtown somewhere. To sleep in a big comfy bed or stay up late watching movies in the room and ordering room service. Maybe sneaking away to jump in the pool or hot tub! Yes, the hot tub would be even better.

I would much rather drink a glass of juice or milk, or snack on pecans and cheese all day, than eat a full meal. In fact, there are few things I love more than cheese.

I absolutely love reading! It is one of my all-time favorite things to do. If the weather is nice and the sun is shining, I could sit outdoors forever and just read. And I mostly read classic literature and non-fiction than anything else…though occasionally it is fun to read one of the silly paperbacks that Aunt Zoe gives me when I see her. I can usually finish one of those in a few hours, which can be a nice break from the heady books I tend to read, and usually makes me feel like the fastest reader in the world!

Anytime I see Meryl Streep in a movie it makes me want to be an actor. And the idea of being able to someday introduce myself as a writer thrills me like nothing else! Except maybe being able to say I am a linguist and a writer…who just finished filming a new movie with my dear friend and mentor, Meryl!

Me Too, Jesus! Me Too!

Meagan E. Ahlstrom

I have done so much reading lately! I don't remember the last time I really had a chance to just read. Or I should say, I don't know when was the last time I made time for myself to read. The last time was…a lifetime ago. And I have so many great books that I have never even opened! But now! Now, I make time to read again. I make time for me, which is fairly easy to do since I have so much time to myself nowadays. ☺ Regardless, I am already on my third novel since the very end of December, and it feels great!

(Side-note: I love pink! Man, how could I have forgotten how much I LOVE the color pink!)

I don't want to miss out on this time of being young. I mean, my whole life is ahead of me. I can make all my dreams come true. I just have to be true to myself and to my heart.

God knows. He knows exactly what He has planned for my life, for my future. And for some reason, I feel like it puts a big smile on His face just thinking about it! ☺

Me too, Jesus! Me too! ☺

Psalm 108:1-5

My heart, O God, is steadfast;
    I will sing and make music with all my soul.

Awake, harp and lyre!
    I will awaken the dawn.

I will praise You, Lord, among the nations;
    I will sing of You among the peoples.

For great is Your love, higher than the heavens;
    Your faithfulness reaches to the skies.

Be exalted, O God, above the heavens;
    let Your glory be over all the earth.

Court Jester

Rebecca L. Ahlstrom

So many times through the years when Meagan would have me or our family laughing, I would jokingly say something like, "I don't think even God knows what to do with you." She would inevitably respond, "Me and God...we are like this." And she would hold up two fingers and then cross them, and follow up by saying, "I make God laugh!" (I so admired that—how comfortable she was in her relationship with Christ.)

Through this long and painful journey, I have thought MUCH and read books on life after death. Although there are strong arguments representing many opinions, I have come to believe in my own heart that Meagan is alive and well...and not "sleeping." Many of you might say that this is a "feel-good" resolve, and it might very well be. But I feel confident of this, God did indeed enjoy Meagan's humor. After all, He created it. He created her.

Meagan knew on this earth that her humor entertained God. On a few occasions, she described herself as His "court jester." Oh, if you could have the memories our family has—her humorous interpretive dance, her conversations in other accents, the operatic songs she would mimic, the celebrities she would imitate, or the really, really high-pitched voices she would use to talk to our dogs or the animals she would come in contact with (even cows or horses she would call out to as we drove by). She never seemed to run out of "material." And on the serious side, if you could have heard the sounds of her worshiping her Lord in her room with full surrender, or the passion I would see in her eyes when she talked about Him, or the prayers she would pray as though He were sitting right there with her!

In my sad hours, and there are many, I can quickly think of Meagan's smile or her humor...and warmth fills my heart. There's a place deep in me where I have no doubt that although she made us laugh here on earth, surely He created her for such a time as this—for His pleasure, His laughter, His entertainment. I am sure she is not alone. I am sure she is among many. And tonight, I choose to rest my heart on the thought that Meagan is somewhere in His courts— singing to the One she loves, and of course…making Him laugh!

(Meag, I still hear the sounds of your laughter!)

Psalm 139:13-14

For You created my inmost being;
  You knit me together in my mother's womb.

I praise You because I am fearfully and wonderfully made;
  Your works are wonderful,
  I know that full well.

I Was Dying, and It Was an Incredible Day!

Meagan E. Ahlstrom

Yesterday it rained. It was one of those perfect rains, too. Not too windy. Not too hard. Just slow, big, big drops. One of those rains where it was useless to even run to your car or your next class because the drops were so big you would only make it worse by moving faster! And it smelled incredible! Fresh and clean with a hint of fall. It was perfect. I skipped my last class and walked to my car just so I could have a reason to walk across campus. I enjoyed every second of that walk!

It was hilarious watching all the prissy little girls running for cover and the people who had umbrellas walking right beside them offering no help. I was amazed how many guys with umbrellas I passed on my way to the car. And not a single one offered me his umbrella or even to walk with me! You know, had it been 40 years ago, they would have been laying down the shirt off their back just so I wouldn't get my shoes wet! I could see it in their eyes, too. Every single one I passed looked at me soaking wet with an "Oops" smile on my face, knowing they should probably be a gentleman and offer some assistance. But with every look of concern, a fear of tardiness seemed to soon follow. Oh well.

I stopped at the light, waiting to cross, soaking wet with my hair plastered to my face. A girl walked up behind me, waiting for the light as well. She had an umbrella. I waited for her to ask if I wanted to wait for the light with her under her blue and white striped shelter. And as the sign across the street blinked "WALK," I realized I was still waiting. Waiting until I saw her walk right past me! Not that

I was so concerned with someone sharing their cover and saving me from the position I chose to put myself in. I was enjoying the rain! It was beautiful! I was just amazed at how many people walked by without caring about one other person. Not to toot my own horn, but I would have offered to walk with anyone who forgot their umbrella, had I remembered mine! ☺

As I made my way to the car, I began walking slower. Here I was, laughing at myself for so enjoying something that everyone around me seemed to be running away from. I kept thinking about how I would act if I knew I was dying and only had six months to live. With that thought in mind, I approached my car, threw my book bag in, and stood in the rain. Arms outstretched and face to the sky, just like in the movies! It was slightly sunny outside, and that smell! You can't beat that smell! I heard cars rolling by me as I faced the grass in front of me, my back to the rest of the parking lot. I could picture everyone wondering what in the world I was doing. But it didn't bother me. Who cares what people say? For that one moment, I was dying. Dying from something awful. Something incurable. And appreciating the rain and everything around me. Loving life. And loving every second of it!

I shook my hair out like a wet dog. I looked down at my brand new purple cashmere cardigan that was now soaked beyond recognition, tapped my black pumps in the large puddle I was standing in, noticed my pants were wet to mid-shin, laughed, and then got in my car to drive away. I knew I had a few errands to run before going home but realized I looked like a woman who just thawed from being frozen for a hundred years in a block of ice. I was about to pass the store, too worried about what people would think, when I remembered—I was dying, and it was an incredible day! I was happy. And with that, I pulled out the day's To-Do-List. I returned home a while later, with every task scratched off. ☺

I told Ashlea about my day later that afternoon and about how not one boy chose to be a gentleman. We talked about that subject for quite a while. I told her how I was so worked up that I decided when I got to my car that I was going to pull my umbrella out of the back seat and pass it through my window to the first person I saw victim to the rain. She asked, "Well, did you?" I told her, "No. I pulled right out of that parking lot and thought the same thing probably every single guy I passed thought: 'I'm gonna need my umbrella tomorrow.'" She laughed. I didn't feel that bad, however, since literally every person I did pass pulling out of the parking lot either had an umbrella or was wearing a baseball cap. Then it hit me—maybe everyone that passed wasn't saying they were going to need their umbrella tomorrow. The thought that crossed their minds was probably more along the lines of, "Poor thing. Sucks she didn't check the weather." ☺

Finally

Meagan E. Ahlstrom

I need to scream.
I need to laugh.
I want to cry.
Yet all I seem to do is continually ask, "Why?"

It seems I have waited for so, so long!
The minutes were hours.
The days became years.
Never knowing when it would come here.

Now that I have it,
I don't know what to think
Or how to feel.
I simply wonder, "Is this seriously for real?"

Along with tears from me,
A million questions flow.
Questions of "Why me?"
With answers I may never know.

Regardless of how confusing
Or strange things may seem,
I feel it is good!
I know it is good!
Therefore, God, thank you for blessing me!!!!!!!

Guidance, Please

Meagan E. Ahlstrom

Lord, I need some guidance. I don't even know what I should be doing right now, or in my future. I mean, I know how I want my future to look, but I don't know how to get there. Lord, please give me guidance. Show me where to go, what I should be, and what I should be doing. Help me get focused, please.

I feel like 90% of what I write is uncertainty. I wonder when it will be that I actually write something about my life that is clear. How many days, weeks, or years from now? I suppose...we will see. In the meantime, I'll keep waiting. And praying. ALWAYS, ALWAYS PRAYING. Lord, give me guidance, please. May I please have Your favor in my job, with my life, Lord, please. Favor. Guidance. Grace. Please.

John 14:15, 21

"If you love me, you will obey what I command.... Those who know my commands and obey them are the ones who love me, and my Father will love those who love me. I will love them and will show myself to them." (NCV) OBEY THE LORD.

Isaiah 30:21

Whether you turn to the right or to the left, your ears will hear a voice behind you, saying, "This is the way; walk in it."

Before We Ever Got Lost

Rebecca L. Ahlstrom

I have been asked to share "our story" again at one of the high schools; however, this will be the first display of our crashed vehicle, which will be on the premises in a strategic location. I have not seen the vehicle or photos of it...until this past Monday (in prep for seeing the "real" thing next Friday).

Nothing could have prepared me for seeing the photo. I have done everything to AVOID seeing the car, until now where I find myself in a Catch-22. I have no descriptive words except to say, "Seeing the photo messed me up." Emotions are swirling inside me, underlined with questions. In my distress, I recall a silly memory of Meagan and me in the vehicle just about a month before the tragedy, and a revelation I would like to share that has since come from it:

After Meagan got off work, she came with me to run an errand. We got to our destination fine, but on the way home I thought I knew a shortcut. Well, we ended up miles in the wrong direction surrounded by barren cornfields. It was dusk, warm outside, windows and sunroof open, and I didn't see that the road ahead of us came to a completely unexpected end! I was only going 30 mph, but Meagan and I screamed loudly at the same time! She screamed noticing the road's end. I screamed because there were about 8 to 10 deer to the right of us. I couldn't believe it! They were beautiful! I slammed on my brakes and turned my car slightly so my headlights would shine on them. There they were, just staring back at us as if to say, "What?!"

Meagan slapped my leg and called me a crazy kook, which I deserved, BUT the deer were just gorgeous and they didn't run away. I couldn't believe it!

If you know Meagan, this is when she got all Bronx on me (and I mean that in the most endearing way) and said almost verbatim, "Our front wheels are in a cornfield, and you are drooling over deer! Rebecca, I swear, when you're old and can't take care of yourself so you're living with me in my mansion, I'm going to wheel you out into the middle of a field every morning, tie corncobs to your wrists and ankles and put peanut butter all over your lips and let you sit out there all day long. Then when I come home at the end of the day, I'll wheel you back knowing that you were happy in deer heaven and that I served you well!"

I busted up laughing at her humor but also because 1) I thought I seriously might enjoy that, and 2) I loved how she always said she would take care of Leo and me when we become old and feeble—but always with a Meagan twist.

Anyway, after blasting me, she leaned halfway out the open window and began talking to the deer in a British accent until she caught eyes with one that she swore was about ready to attack. We sped away, laughing at ourselves, and she called me a crazy kook a few more times.

Still in unfamiliar territory, we realized the only way to get our bearings was to go back where we came from—before we ever got lost. We made it home finally, but what should have taken us 30 minutes round trip took us way over an hour. Regardless, we made it home.

This morning I realized how significant (beyond the humor) the event is to this unwanted journey I find myself on. When I battle day after day the thoughts of the crash and losing Meagan; when great sorrow fills my soul so I cannot even see past my own pain; and confusion and uncertainty cloud my vision so I cannot see the path HE has laid before me—sometimes I remember to "go back to before I was ever lost." And when I make the effort, it is there that I find my Father's arms…and I am home.

Matthew 6:6

But when you pray, go into your room, close the door and pray to your Father, who is unseen. Then your Father, who sees what is done in secret, will reward you.

My Room

Meagan E. Ahlstrom

When I was younger, I'd go to school, face the world, fight my battles, and worry about whatever, but I always knew that once I was on my way home—I was home free. Nothing I went through that day mattered once I entered my sanctuary, my house, my home, my refuge.

Where is my sanctuary now? My room! Every day, every single day, I am told to sit and talk. I soooo love those talks, and I love how He listens. He knows everything. He knows what I go through, and He knows how to help me through it. And boy, how He loves me! No matter what I tell Him, no matter how much wrong I've done, He still forgives me. We really don't even have to talk; just knowing I am His is something—something amazing. But those talks…how I love our talks. And I love how He changed me. Even through all my complaining and lack of understanding—He loves me. And though I still have a lot of learning and changing to do, I know that He will always be with me and He will guide me.

Knowing I am headed home and seeing my room is something I can't wait to do. Actually, it's having those talks that I really look forward to. I don't know why I feel Him so close in my room because He is everywhere, but He feels so near in my room.

Look! He's done it again. He has turned my depression into happiness, my anguish into light. And that's what He is…my light…The Light. And that's what I am…HAPPY!

2 Samuel 22:29

You, Lord, are my lamp;
    the Lord turns my darkness into light.

The Silence of Light

Rebecca L. Ahlstrom

I met a precious new friend today. Her name is Barb. And she gave me permission to share this story.

The story actually begins two years ago. Barb had recently lost her husband after a long illness. Months following, in December, she tragically lost her son she loved so deeply. Adam was 24. Her life was shattered. And she found herself alone in what used to be a full and lively home—clinging to her faith in God.

After grieving deeply for both of them for months, she decided to "venture out into Von Maur and just wander around. It was my first time out...just to be 'out.'" While walking around the store, she became overwhelmed and began crying. She said a beautiful young lady came to her and invited her to sit at the cosmetics counter—a young lady named Meagan Ahlstrom. She added that Meagan wiped away her tears as Barb shared her story. They both cried. Barb said that Meagan then shared "her story and how much she loved her family." Barb went back to visit Meagan a few times because "it felt so good to talk with her," and added that she was amazed Meagan was not shaken by her emotions or her pain—but was just very compassionate and seemed older than her years.

Then...June happened—our worst nightmare. Barb was shocked and heartsick at the news.

After the memorial service, Barb sent Leo and me a card. It had our attention from the moment we opened it because on the front of the card was written the exact quote by Thomas Moore that Leo recited at Meagan's Memorial Celebration: "Earth has no sorrow that heaven cannot heal." Our hearts were captivated at what we read—that Barb had suffered such loss and through her loss had come to know our daughter and was deeply touched by her life. And now Barb, through this story, has deeply touched ours. Her card ends, "My life is full of thanksgiving. I am thankful that I had those few times with your precious daughter." Leo and I were moved to tears—to hear of yet another account of Meagan just being "Meagan" and loving people. How ironic that Meagan was comforting someone, not knowing she would soon be in Heaven. And believe as you choose; Barb and I feel that since both Meagan and Adam were/are "believers," they have already met and Meagan was able to share a mother's heart to her son that she lost so quickly. Barb and I cried together. And then we talked about HOPE.

Romans 8:38-39

For I am convinced that neither death nor life, neither angels nor demons, neither the present nor the future, nor any powers, neither height nor depth, nor anything else in all creation, will be able to separate us from the love of God that is in Christ Jesus our Lord.

Jesus, You Are

Meagan E. Ahlstrom

Lord, I heard Your answer: "Seek Me and you WILL be over it." Seek You and it will be in the past. You are right, and I know exactly what I am supposed to do. If I seek You, pray to You, spend time with You, I will be too focused on my relationship with You and what You are doing in my life and what You have planned for my future to care about the past or let worldly things bother me. You are right, Lord. I want to know You more than ever before.

I love You, Lord. You are my everything. Everything good that is in me or in my life is You or because of You. Thank You, God, for loving me so much.

Jesus, You ARE my best friend.

Sometimes...Just Because

Meagan E. Ahlstrom

I believe a young girl in love is a very delicate being. We love so differently than men. Wholeheartedly, sacrificing so much of ourselves for the happiness of another. Convincing ourselves every day that the pain is temporary, and that our efforts, our devotion will pay off. That it will all work out in the end for something that will last a lifetime.

We genuinely believe that the love we feel for another human being could actually change him, make him better, and help him see the light. And every day that it doesn't occur is just another day to try harder—only to fail again.

What is it in us that allows us to love another more than ourselves, constantly forgiving the faults of another, which only leads to the destruction of our own hearts? And why is it that we never seem to learn?

Even when we find ourselves separated from the situation, it still consumes our every thought, altering the way we live our lives, forcing us to hold on to something that isn't even present, crippling us in our weak attempts to move on with our lives. And even separated, we find we are in no better situation, continually playing the game over in our head: "Which is worse—dying inside in the company of an indifferent witness or dying inside where no one can see?"

You say easily it's the latter, but with the former there are at least bleak, momentary instances of happiness that perpetually torture you yet also never fail to convince you that all the pain is worth it…for that one look, that one touch, that one moment.

And you begin to hate yourself for your weakness. You begin to hate yourself before ever recognizing the wrong in the other person.

I could easily forgive a man for hurting me who did not realize what he was doing—before I could forgive a man who knew precisely the consequences of his actions and chose to do them anyway.

So, what is there to love in a man like that? What forces us to hold on with all our might? "Because it wasn't always that bad." Because we never believe that the bad in a person could outweigh the good. Because we believe people can change and genuinely want to be better. Because we believe that love really does last a lifetime—even if it's not a perfect love.

And sometimes…just because.

Patiently Waiting

Meagan E. Ahlstrom

Well, it's right after 11pm. I just got in bed and have officially made it through another day.

It is a lot easier than it would have been a year or two ago, but it still consumes my every thought.

Kelly told me today how proud she is of me. How I deserve so much better. That's exactly what Ashley said the other day, too. And although I agree that I deserve better, I cannot say that it is not still difficult.

But I will survive. I believe I am in better hands. That God knows exactly what He is doing with and in my life. And I trust Him. I do trust You, Lord.

I don't exactly know what You have for me, but I know, as always, it will be for the best!

So in the meantime, I will be patient. I am waiting on You, Lord. I am patiently waiting.

Think About It

Meagan E. Ahlstrom

Is who you really are…
What you really look like…
How he sees you?
Or when you cry,
Even about the stupidest things,
Does he cry with you?
Contrary to what some of your friends think,
He actually does cry!
And with you!
And he has this ability
Even when you are crying,
And he is right there crying with you.
In the midst of your pain,
He somehow has the strength
To not pick himself back up
But to pick you up with him!
And no matter how much you cry
Or how sad you get,
He always makes you laugh.
It's hard to believe that such a relationship
Or such an incredible being could actually exist.
But it does.
He does!
And there is no man or thing
That could ever or will ever take his place.

For He is God!
And none can compare!

Smack Me in the Face

Meagan E. Ahlstrom

Lord, I love You.

It depends on the level of one's relationship with You, but I love how everything that I have planned for MY life—everything that I try to do in MY will—You smack me in the face with and remind me once again just WHO's in control! An answer to my prayers—ALWAYS remind me WHO's in control and by whatever means!

I love You, Lord!

Romans 11:33-36

Oh, the depth of the riches of the wisdom and
  knowledge of God!
   How unsearchable His judgments,
   and His paths beyond tracing out!

"Who has known the mind of the Lord?
  Or who has been His counselor?"

"Who has ever given to God,
  that God should repay them?"

For from Him and through Him and for Him are all things.
  To Him be the glory forever! Amen.

High-Heeled Kick to the Backside

Rebecca L. Ahlstrom

Years ago, I led the women's ministry for our church in Tennessee. We met every Wednesday night in our home. Since I felt this ministry was a "God directive," I wanted every meeting to be, well…God-directed. I would spend hours in preparation praying and seeking God and pleading. Sure, anyone could come up with a short "message" to share in the meeting. Anyone could create a group discussion. But I knew in my heart that God required something more of me for this season. I knew He wanted full dependence on Him. And I was determined to walk that out. So each week I pursued Him like a nursing calf after its momma.

There is one Wednesday during the initial weeks that I remember particularly well. I was working overtime in a high-stress executive job, and as usual, I rushed home to clean the downstairs for my visitors, walk the dogs, feed my family, prepare snacks and coffee…and tweak my notes for the meeting. But this week, God inspired in me NO message. He gave me NOTHING! All my pleading all week…NOTHING! All my desperate pursuing…NOTHING! And now, I was down to the last half hour. Women would be showing up at my home "expecting"…and I had NOTHING! I was empty.

So I did what any normal woman in this predicament would do—I PANICKED!! I went a little crazy for just a few minutes, shouting insanities like, "What am I doing! I am not qualified to lead this group. I have nothing to offer these ladies. Who do I think I am?" And my heart sank in despair.

Meagan walked in the house at that wonderfully impressive moment. My daughter, who exuded spiritual confidence on a level I had yet to attain, proceeded with the verbal spanking, "Geez, Mom! You need to sign up for my self-esteem class." And she exited upstairs.

In that one moment, the heaviness cleared. In that one moment, I saw myself as she did. And it was not a pretty sight. But I did not feel defeated. Actually, quite the opposite—I laughed! Because there it was—my message! And delivered by my daughter's high-heeled shoe to my backside! My message: our identity is in Christ alone and not through our own efforts. Through our emptiness, His glory is revealed. Through our weakness, He is made strong. And...insecurities are ONLY insecurities IF we give them power!

2 Corinthians 12:9

But He said to me, "My grace is sufficient for you, for My power is made perfect in weakness." Therefore I will boast all the more gladly about my weaknesses, so that Christ's power may rest on me.

Just Show Up

Meagan E. Ahlstrom

My lease is up at the end of July. And unless something huge happens here in the next three months, I am moving. I'm moving to Chicago. I miss my family. And my heart feels pulled to that church, which is a great "pro" of moving there. It's exciting. Just thinking about doing something totally different, even something scary, is very exciting!

I feel so much of my last few years have been in the same place. Same situation with school. Worrying over the same boy. No true creative outlet. I feel that changing location will change a lot for me.

I originally thought I would work for Lauder/Dillard's until they transferred me somewhere else, but that somewhere else just isn't getting here soon enough. Honestly, I want to live in a hundred different places. And if I am going to do that, I need to start now!

Granted...more than that, I want the Lord's timing. I want what You have for my life, Lord. I want the life You have for me.

I am reading, or I should say re-reading, "The Papa Prayer," which I started I suppose a year ago. It's funny how I feel like I can't pray until I finish it, or like I am not doing it "right" so I need to learn how to pray before I can! When really, I am sure the Lord just loves having me SHOW UP. So, I am going to hold tight to that idea and pray as much as I feel like it! ☺

Lord, may I do what's best by You. I love You. You are my whole heart, Jesus. Keep me strong. Keep me focused. Forgive me for all my sins, Lord. Forgive me for every time I dishonored You. For every time I was not obedient, forgive me, please. I will be strong to live a better life for You. Amen! Amen! Amen! I love You, Lord!

Plans that Will Blow My Mind

Meagan E. Ahlstrom

Lord, I need Your help, and I need Your guidance. Father, please show me the steps I am supposed to take. Help me understand and clearly see my calling. Please, Lord, guide my steps. Show me the path You want me to take so that I may fulfill my calling and Your will for my life. I don't want to settle, Lord. I don't want to simply do what's right in front of me.

Lord, I feel deep in my soul that You have huge plans for my future. Plans that will blow my mind and force me to fall on my face in thanksgiving! Jesus, I know You do. I have no idea just how You want me to get there, or what it is exactly You want me to do, but I know it is going to be bigger than I could ever imagine. I know it is going to greatly affect my parents and Aaron and Mel. And I know it is going to affect millions.

Help me, Lord. May I have a clear vision, a strong spirit, and a Christ-like heart in every way. Help me, Lord.

Be with my family and loved ones tonight. Give them wonderful dreams and may they see You as they sleep. Protect them, wherever they are.

Greatness Is Coming

Meagan E. Ahlstrom

There is something inside. Something constant. Always present. Always searching.

It is something that knows far more than me. Something that can see things I cannot see, and feel things I cannot explain.

Something inside me. It is a feeling that accepts nothing less than greatness. That believes in the impossible. And has unsurpassable amounts of hope…faith.

There is no guessing. No questions. Through my mind, my doubt, my heart, my hurt…it is the feeling…this something inside that is sure…completely certain… reassuring every other part of me of what it already knows. There is greatness. And it is coming.

Greatness…is coming.

Habakkuk 3:1-2

Lord, I have heard of Your fame;
   I stand in awe of Your deeds, Lord.

Repeat them in our day,
   in our time make them known;
   in wrath remember mercy.

Purpose

Rebecca L. Ahlstrom

"…You are on the path of MY choosing, so do not give up! Hope in Me, for you will again praise Me for the help of My Presence."

These last few years have obviously been very difficult. My family has suffered much. Leo and I have served and loved the Lord for 30+ years, and now we have been "pressed but not crushed, persecuted but not abandoned, struck down but not destroyed." Speaking for me, everything I "knew" was tossed like chaff. My faith has been tested in ways I never dreamed. For years, I even doubted that God loved me and was with me. After all, why did the One that my family trusted allow this tragedy to befall us? The "whys" consume my thoughts.

My journey has been a cry for purpose. PURPOSE! Why had God left me "here"? I can't just exist! Surely GOD didn't let me go through HELL to just leave me here. I need PURPOSE more than I need food! So I cry and plead and beg and spend hours every day just being with God, My Only Hope.

All that pleading…He heard me! God has opened the door for me to share our story, and then soon word got out, and the invitations continue to fall in my lap. From high schools, to regular opportunities in a packed courtroom of DUI offenders, to church opportunities, to public appearances…HUGE PURPOSE!

Meagan had the gift of public speaking and performing before crowds. She loved center stage. So with each opportunity to share our story, I strategically step into a pair of her shoes (and she has many) and ask God for every ounce of her gift of speaking He would give me.

Though I pray for it desperately every day, He has been faithful to give me PURPOSE, but I have paid the ultimate price. Yet from my mouth today let the words flow, "...I am on the path of HIS choosing, so I will not give up! My hope is in You, and I praise You for the help of Your Presence." For surely You are my source of strength at each high school, at each courthouse, at each event, in each personal conversation...and this morning I woke up with a thankful heart for the first time since the crash.

He kept His promise to me: "Commit your way to the Lord; trust in Him and He will do this: He will make your righteousness shine like the dawn, the justice of your cause like the noonday sun." (Psalm 37:5-6, NIV (Zondervan)) I will continue to share our story of tragedy and redemption to glorify my Father and honor our daughter.

Lord, let me not waste a day. Let me not miss an opportunity. Let me be sure to listen for Your voice. Regardless of the condition of my heart, please use me.

Psalm 138:8

The Lord will vindicate me;
   Your love, Lord, endures forever—
   do not abandon the works of Your hands.

The New Has Come

Meagan E. Ahlstrom

As Christians we are called to follow Christ, to lead by His example, to live a life that honors Him, pleases Him. We are called to be obedient. I want my life to be pleasing to the Lord; therefore, it is only fitting that I would also want a relationship that pleases God.

Along with James 3:17 (ESV), "But the wisdom of above is first pure, then peaceable, gentle, open to reason, full of mercy and good fruits, impartial and sincere", I have been focusing on a few other Scriptures that are helping me pray in a very specific way. The first one is 1 Corinthians 6:18-20 (ESV): "Flee from sexual immorality. Every other sin a person commits is outside the body, but the sexually immoral person sins against his own body. Or do you not know that your body is a temple of the Holy Spirit within you, whom you have from God? You are not your own, for you were bought with a price. So glorify God in your body."

This Scripture really moves me. Sometimes I choose not to acknowledge that I am a temple for the Holy Spirit! But I am!! We all are—for those of us who love Christ!

I want to honor Him not only with my mind but also with my heart. Not only with my words but with my actions, with my body. Life is not worth living without Jesus, without thanking God and living a life that reflects Him and His love. After all, in The Great Commission, Matthew 28:16-20, Christ calls us as disciples to go and make disciples, to spread the Good News to all nations. And how can we do that if we do not live a life that first pleases God, and then also reflects Him?

I believe that anytime we choose to do our own thing and take our focus off of Jesus, the enemy wins. He then has a hold on us, ruining our relationships with others, and creating an obstacle in our relationship with Jesus. We must be watchful of these traps and also choose to honor God with our love.

Last but not least, Philippians 4:8-9 (ESV): "Finally, brothers, whatever is true, whatever is honorable, whatever is just, whatever is pure, whatever is lovely, whatever is commendable, if there is any excellence, if there is anything worthy of praise, think about these things. What you have learned and received and heard and seen in me—practice these things, and the God of peace will be with you."

If we seek and focus on the Lord, we will see the Lord in all we do. We will have His peace. We will be at peace. May we truly honor Him in all we do. Amen!

2 Corinthians 5:17 (ESV): "Therefore, if anyone is in Christ, he is a new creation. The old is passed away; behold, the new has come." May we be in Christ—a new creation!

Lady in Waiting

Meagan E. Ahlstrom

…On another note, the chapter I read today in "Lady in Waiting" was "Lady of Virtue." The end of the chapter homework suggested I read Proverbs 31 and ask the Lord to show me one quality I need to develop (discipline, graciousness, diligence), and then to focus on and pray over that quality for an entire month before asking the Lord to show me another one.

I am excited about this task! What a good idea! I want to be a Proverbs 31 woman for God, for myself. My whole reason for reading this book so slowly is so that I can meditate on what I read and truly apply it to my life—that also goes for my Bible study time.

I want to be the best I can be, the woman God has called me to be, and I know this will not be an overnight development. This taking one virtue at a time for a month deal is right down my alley. I'm going to make a list of the qualities but study the whole chapter, and then let the Lord speak to me about which virtue to pray over first, then second, and so on.

Man, I am at such an exciting place in my life. It's such a wonderful feeling—this improving myself, seeking the will of God business!!

Running Out of Time

Meagan E. Ahlstrom

I was talking to Mom tonight about work and life and love. I want to finish school, I told her. I want to master and complete my foreign language studies. I want to travel. I want to live in a hundred different cities. I want to be ridiculously successful and very wealthy…OR, very successful and ridiculously wealthy. Ha!

We discussed how I feel so old. Like 23 is too old to do some of the things I want to do—AS IF I AM RUNNING OUT OF TIME!

Mom was trying to explain to me that I can do anything I want. Just to continue to work hard, stay focused, and plan. Plan to finish school, how and when, and then do it! Plan to travel. Take some vacation days. Save some money. Then do it! She said I just need to be a little more well-rounded. Make sure that I am staying busy in things outside of work. Things I value. Things that will challenge me and that I find rewarding.

I know this. I've known this. But it was interesting to hear from her.

She said that she would love for me to finish school. That she believes me completing school will really satisfy me, but that I can do it and still keep this job [Manager, Estée Lauder]. The opportunities with this job are endless. And it is such an unbelievable blessing right now. I really don't want to sacrifice that and throw away all my hard work just because I am getting restless.

But I'll have to do it the old-fashioned way—by taking it one day at a time. It's almost midnight, so I guess today was somewhat of a success. ☺ I guess.

More Movement

Meagan E. Ahlstrom

Lord, I need You. I trust You and Your spirit in me that keeps me on track. Lord, please give me guidance on how to handle this next step in my life. I need more movement, Lord, please! More movement!

I don't like this still place. This hold on me keeping me in one place. But show me. If You would have me here longer, I will be patient. I am no quitter, but I will do what's best for my life.

I don't want to make a foolish decision based on uncertain circumstances that I cannot trust because of all the underlying emotion. I want solid direction. I want to know in my head and heart what I should do!

Only Your best, Lord. Only Your best! Please, Father God!

The Woman Within

Meagan E. Ahlstrom

"It doesn't matter where your hidden inadequacies come from. God's grace is greater than them all." (*The Woman Within* by Vonette Bright)

How funny is it that I know I am capable of great things, and yet because of that, am fearful of acting on the desires of my heart? How funny or maybe how foolish? I don't know why it is, Lord, that I can be so afraid at times to do good things, and afraid to commit to do good things. So I fill my life with such meaninglessness that I am miserable, and worse, bear no good fruit.

I realize I am known, recognized, and judged by the fruit I bear. Help me, Lord. Help me reject the useless, meaningless activities in my life that consume so much of my time and energy and that bear no good fruit.

I want to do great things for You and for Your kingdom. I want people to benefit from knowing me. Not because of who I am, but because of who You are in me. I want people to see only good fruit. I want my words and actions to be a reflection of the goodness in my heart—of You in my heart!

Make me aware of all the things in my life that displease You. And forgive me for the things I do that I know displease You.

I want my life to be filled with You. I want to be a better person, friend, daughter, sister, and (one day) an amazing wife to the man You have for me.

How selfish I have been to those close to me! How ridiculous I have been not trying to be the best "me" possible for them. Forgive me, Lord. And help change my heart. Please.

Psalm 61:1-2

Hear my cry, O God;
   listen to my prayer.

From the ends of the earth I call to You,
   I call as my heart grows faint;
   Lead me to the Rock that is higher than I.

The Piano Man

Rebecca L. Ahlstrom

After putting it off for weeks, I left the house today for Von Maur. (Meagan's last place of employment, a family-owned chain, quality similar to Nordstrom's.) Meagan got Leo and me hooked on particular Estée Lauder products years ago, but now pain is associated with the purchase. Today was the day that I pulled up my bootstraps and kicked myself into gear. Yes, I could order online, but I love Von Maur and want to support them. It's a beautiful store, Christian-owned, and their staff and management were so supportive of our family through the tragedy. I have many memories of Meagan there, so I brave Von Maur about every four months and recapture a few, as painful as it is. Today was my day. But today would be different.

I am not usually on that side of town, for obvious reasons. The drive up to Von Maur is agonizing. The walk in is painful. BUT it's the pianist playing the grand piano near the escalators that, without fail, unleashes the floodgates of emotion for me—before I can ever get to the Estée Lauder counter! And I can almost always tell when it is Gary playing before I ever see him. He truly plays from the heart. But the biggest connection is that for the months that Meagan worked for Von Maur, she loved his playing and talked about him regularly. When I would stop by, Meagan would always say, "Mom, think of a song. You've got to stump Gary." That always seemed to be the goal, but I don't believe she ever succeeded. Anyway, it was "their thing."

I never met Gary, a distinguished older man from the Caribbean, personally before today. But in the past I always smiled and complimented his playing by putting my hand over my heart.

Today, after making it to the Estée Lauder counter and purchasing what I needed, I made it down the escalator to the men's department for Leo. I walked by Gary and patted my heart (with tears in my eyes). I could hardly breathe. His beautiful rendition of the old classics reminded me so much of Meagan. I kept walking.

I bought Leo a couple of shirts and walked toward the escalator to go up and then out. But I couldn't get past Gary. I had been in the store with Meagan as she would try to stump him or as she would applaud him from over the balcony like a princess. But today was my first day to personally meet him when I approached him and asked if he remembered my daughter.

After expressing deep sympathies, he lit up. He commented on how Meagan always wore black—black EVERYTHING—and how it made her look so dramatic. (I guess she never bothered to tell him it was her uniform dress.) He recalled the last time he saw Meagan. She leaned over the upstairs balcony with gentle applause, pleased with his performance, so he pointed up at her and said, "This one's for you!" and played the old classic, "When I Fall in Love." He said she just loved it! They talked later, but that was the last time he saw her before our fatal trip to Nashville the next day. And he said he will never forget it. He told me how, though he didn't know her well, he loved seeing her pass by because she was always smiling and would wave while going up the escalator to her counter or gently applaud his playing. He said she had something special. She was beautiful inside and out, and she had a presence about her that was different. When he returned to work on Monday after the tragedy and was told the news by management, he excused himself, went to the men's room, and was moved to tears.

We talked for a minute more, and then he asked, "Let me play something for YOU...anything." I honestly could hear Meagan laughing and saying, "Stump him, Mom! Stump him!" But all I wanted was to relive that last song he played for her. So I made my request known. He smiled such a warm smile and then said, "I'm going to play this with Meagan in mind." He sat quietly in deep thought for almost a minute before proceeding. I stood near the piano.

Though crying, I realized I was missing a huge opportunity so I recorded the end of his performance. I cut him off too soon because when he finished the song, he turned around, pointed up, and said, "THAT was for your beautiful Meagan." Oh, my heart! Oh, my Meagan!!

He gave me one of his cards and I gave him one of the Meagan Facebook cards. He said, "Ahhh...there's that beautiful face." I hugged him and said how much he blessed me today, and I walked off toward the escalators trying to make it outside. Then my spirit recognized a familiar sound! It was "Amazing Grace." As I was going up, I looked down, and he whispered, "This is for you!" My tears flowed. No holding back. I noticed a gentleman walk over to him. Gary looked up at me and said, "He knew your daughter too!" I couldn't speak. The hymn rang into the depths of my soul.

When I got to the top, I leaned over the glass railing like Meagan must have done a hundred times before, and I patted my heart with tears streaming down my face. "Thank you" managed to form on my lips...but no audible words. I just kept patting my heart. I walked outside, sat in my car...and cried. And then I managed a whisper to God, "Thank You for that gift."

Deuteronomy 7:9

Know therefore that the Lord your God is God; He is the faithful God, keeping His covenant of love to a thousand generations of those who love Him and keep His commandments.

Only Your Best

Meagan E. Ahlstrom

Lord, You know how much I need You. Even when I don't acknowledge it, don't admit it, and don't even say it out loud. I need You. You are all I have. You are all that is worth having. And I will need You always.

I want Your best, Lord. In all aspects of my life. In all areas. In all ways. I want only Your best, Lord.

I believe "you only love God as much as you obey Him. Despite all you claim, despite all your obvious actions, you only love God as much as you obey Him!"

It's an amazing feeling—feeling that You are always on my side. You always have my back. And You are absolutely always there for me.

I am getting out of Your way. I am getting out of my own way. And I refuse to listen to any of the lies of the enemy. I know better! I was taught to know better!

Only Your best, Lord.

Sea of Lies

Meagan E. Ahlstrom

It is a strange feeling being on this side of things. A few years ago I would fly to Chicago as much as possible, it seems at least once a month. Many times it was my saving grace. I was able to steal away for the weekend, momentarily escaping the constant struggles that existed in my life at the time, all the while trying to pretend that my life was genuinely good.

I really shouldn't be so hard on myself. I was in school, and I was working…off and on, at least. But I was still struggling to swim in the sea of lies that tried to viciously drown me every day.

Now I am in a very different situation—an almost complete opposite one, really. I am in Chicago now making trips back to Nashville. I am in school, slowly but surely trying to finish. I am working all the time, so much that it unfortunately leaves little time for anything else. I also have my feet planted firmly on very dry land. Not only far away from deceptive, destructive waters—but I am realizing that "sea" no longer exists. Thank You, Jesus.

Some People

Meagan E. Ahlstrom

The world—
Some find pleasure in it;
I find none.
Some find joy in it;
I find none.

Some people submit to depression;
I never do.
Some people live in hatred;
I never do.

Some people are searching;
Some people are hurting;
Some people feel a void;
I know not one of these.

I find pleasure in God.
I find satisfaction in Him.
My life is filled with His joy.
I live surrounded in His love.

I am not searching;
I have been found.
I am not hurting;
I have been healed.
I am not lacking;
I am complete.
I am not of this world;
I am simply in it.
I do not just hear His Word;
Through Him—I live it!

An Entirely New Creation

Meagan E. Ahlstrom

So much of my thinking those years before was all about me! It was very selfish. So much of what mattered to me then was how I felt, how I viewed things, how things would affect me. But that poison does not exist in my heart anymore.

Jesus has created a new thing in me. I truly feel that way. I can see it!

I can't even think of things years ago without shaking my head in disbelief. That just couldn't have been me. How could I allow myself to suffer such things, to stumble so hard, to fall so far?

When the Apostle Paul speaks about how we are a new creation in Christ, it is not just a statement or a heavenly attribute. It's a feeling! I am a walking testament to that Scripture! My past isn't just a past—it was a different life. I am an entirely new creation!

Isaiah 9:2

The people walking in darkness
   have seen a great light;
on those living in the land of deep darkness,
   a light has dawned.

Out of the Wreck I Rise

Rebecca L. Ahlstrom

My Utmost for His Highest is a classic daily devotional by Oswald Chambers. Meagan loved this devotional. She read through it several times over the years and references it in her journals.

After the tragedy I found the book kept by her bed, so I tucked it away for safekeeping—only after I noticed something very profound. Of ALL the devotional days (365 of them!), she dog-eared only ONE—May 19! I have read that marked page many times with so many questions, bewildered by the possibilities. I do not believe in coincidences.

Weeks later, our family headed to south Louisiana to "set" the headstone, which was specially made. The thought of seeing this "image" was almost unbearable. Held by His grace, I paused to recall God's faithfulness…and for whatever reason Meagan marked this page; whatever was going on in her own life at the time, whatever the significance of this one page, I know His fingerprints are evident.

My Utmost for His Highest—May 19th "Out of the Wreck I Rise" begins, "God does not keep His child immune from trouble; He promises, 'I will be with him in trouble…' (Psalm 91:15, ESV). It doesn't matter how real or intense the adversities may be; nothing can ever separate him from his relationship to God. 'In all these things we are more than conquerors…' (Romans 8:37, ESV)." It concludes, "…or else some extraordinary thing happens to someone who holds on to the love of God when the odds are totally against him. Logic is silenced in the face of each of these things which come against him. Only one thing can account for it—the LOVE OF GOD IN CHRIST JESUS."

I believe Meagan was moved to dog-ear this one page and this will always baffle me. The title alone shakes my inner core, for who knows what tomorrow holds but God? Who knows the mind of God…but God? Why was she drawn to this entry? Or why did she end on this entry?

Nonetheless, by His grace, like Meagan, "Out of the wreck I rise!"

2 Samuel 22:17-18, 20

He reached down from on high and took hold of me;
    He drew me out of deep waters.

He rescued me from my powerful enemy,
    from my foes, who were too strong for me.

He brought me out into a spacious place;
    He rescued me because He delighted in me.

Dark Season

Meagan E. Ahlstrom

I was in the darkest season of my life back then. There was hardly any evidence of Christ dwelling within me.

There are events that transpired in those dark days that are so dead to me they will never find new life on pages by my hand. Many things I did that are so foreign to me now. It's as if a completely different person lived my life for those years. Situations I will never write about. Situations that will die with me—having no proof of existence.

It's not that I live in shame or am burdened with regrets. It's just that those things and that person are so far from me. When I look back, it's hard to believe it actually was me.

Yet another reason why I will live my life serving Jesus Christ—my whole life is a testament to His grace and mercy…to His forgiveness and love.

The Life

Meagan E. Ahlstrom

When you find what makes life worth living, you simply have to live for it. It is not a rule, or written that you must do it or die, BUT once you know what really makes life worth anything, your soul, your very being, everything you are has to have it. Without it, there is really no purpose to living. It can be a pretty risky thing, though, because once you know what you've been missing, you tend to get rid of and let go of what you had—at least that's how I see it.

Jesus Christ is life. He is The LIFE. Without Him you can't even experience "life" or even have "life" because you don't have Him. HE is what makes life worth living. Once you know Him, know what you are in Him, and know what He has created you to be, it is hard to go back to what you were. You have a completely different outlook on everything…on LIFE.

To some people that is pretty scary stuff. Some are so comfortable in who they are that it is hard for them to see beyond that—to see beyond into a whole new world of things—a whole new "them." But, in fact, it is not scary at all. God is so amazingly great that life is always an adventure with Him. He makes life worthwhile.

Like I said, He is LIFE. And in my opinion, I would rather live life serving and being with The LIFE than spending all of the time I have been given searching or just not believing.

True Strength

Meagan E. Ahlstrom

I saw a "me" the other day that I had not seen in a very long time. I was weak, Lord. I was needy, and I was weak. However, I don't know if I've ever been truly strong. Maybe distant and emotionally closed off, but never truly strong.

Do I even know what true strength is? I know I am stronger than I used to be. I can see it. And I'll give myself some credit; I am strong, but lately not as strong as I would like to be.

I would like to be strong enough to not let the words of others hurt me. I would like to be strong enough to not need the affirmation and validation of others. More than that, I would like to be strong enough to realize I deserve better when in an unfair situation—with no ifs, ands, or buts about it. Period.

Lord, I need to keep reminding myself everyday—that I am only complete in You and that "true" strength lies only in You. I love You.

Petty Things Are a Waste of My Time

Meagan E. Ahlstrom

Do you think our lives would really be so stressful if we did not partake in the bashing of others or in the spreading of bad news? We are too concerned about what people think about us and not concerned enough about what we think about other people. There are so many hurting, so many struggling to make it through the day, but many of us cannot even see that for we are too worried about what we will wear tomorrow.

I have learned a very important lesson. I don't want to press it upon anyone, yet simply share the joy that I have attained from this newfound conviction: Petty things are a waste of my time. There are bigger things to cry about, and even those things often do not deserve my tears for long.

Maybe I haven't been through what you have been through. But praise the Lord that you are through it and that you have moved on! Maybe I do not have to deal with the situations that you daily have to deal with, but praise the Lord that you are still here and that you have His strength, which forces you to hold on!

I refuse to forget about this conviction, and I promise to hang on to it for as long as I am alive. Along with that promise I make two more: to never underestimate the power and strength that you possess because of our Father who loves us unconditionally, and to never underestimate your wisdom for it is that which possesses you to continue to trust Him. How blessed we are to serve such a compassionate and awesome God, and how merciful He is for allowing us to do so!

You Are the Reason

Meagan E. Ahlstrom

When everything is going wrong,
And I feel like no one cares…
You stand beside me.

When people talk behind my back,
And there's no truth to the smile I wear…
You hold me.

When things seem like they can't get worse,
And I feel I've hit rock bottom…
You console me.

When I've lost my hope,
And misplaced my faith…
You find me.

When I doubt myself,
Feel I'll never succeed…
You make me believe.

When I feel like crying
Over foolish, silly things…
You let me.

When I laugh and am truly happy,
When I have peace and strength…
You are the reason.

No Eye Has Seen

Meagan E. Ahlstrom

Tonight Mom and Dad prayed before they left town. Dad prayed over me the Word, *"No eye has seen, no ear has heard, and no mind has imagined what God has prepared for those who love Him."* 1 Corinthians 2:9 (NLT)

It's true, Lord. I believe that You have blessings in store for us that no eye has ever seen and no ear has ever heard. I believe it.

I once told You that I only want Your best, and I meant it. So, take over, Lord. I trust You. I only want Your best—a life that is phenomenal. A life that helps change the world. A life where no eye has seen and no ear has heard the blessings You have in store for me! Take over, Lord!

Psalm 37:23-24

The Lord makes firm the steps
    of the one who delights in Him;

Though he may stumble, he will not fall,
    for the Lord upholds him with His hand.

Deeper in the Ocean

Rebecca L. Ahlstrom

I found myself in a different situation sharing Meagan's Story/Our Story while on a mission's trip through our church at an English camp in the Czech Republic for people in their 20s. Different because Leo and I weren't leaving directly after as when I spoke at high schools, etc.

No, this time we were staying there on the compound another two days as campers ourselves. People we had lived with, shared meals with, and played games with now had us basically captive. We were approached by a stream of young people with comments, encouragement, discussions, questions, and life-changing stories! PURPOSE!!!! And I tearfully thanked God for the unmerited opportunity.

An emotional conversation with one of the camp leaders left me with a thought I am still processing. As we talked into the late evening, she shared her heart about our story and how it deeply affected her. Tears.

She gently held the Meagan Facebook Group card and poem we made available to the campers, and while looking at them, she said almost verbatim, "Rebecca, if Meagan had not died, I would never have 'met' her or been inspired by her passion for life and for her God. I would never have known about or read her journal entries. Her life, though she impacted many, has now crossed the ocean and is impacting people of the Czech Republic. She reminds me of Emily Dickinson, who never published any of her own writings. They were only published after her death. And over 200 years later, she is still one of the most beloved and well-known poets. THIS is only the beginning."

Meagan wanted to impact her world. Her words echoed loudly in my heart and across the ocean. I cried.

Isaiah 42:16

I will lead the blind by ways they have not known,
  along unfamiliar paths I will guide them;
I will turn the darkness into light before them
  and make the rough places smooth.
These are the things I will do;
  I will not forsake them.

Just Get out of the Way

Meagan E. Ahlstrom

Why? Why can't time move faster? Why when you are hurting does it go by so darn slow? God help me. Please keep me strong.

Okay, so I am reading "The Papa Prayer," and there is a passage I just read that I find very interesting:

"[God] wants me to be as happy as He can make me. And I'm realizing for that to happen, I must give up on the happiness I can find elsewhere."

Interesting. And very true. Since when have any of us ever known what we really wanted? So, if I don't really know, which I really don't, how am I supposed to know what would make me happy? How in the world do I know what will make me happy?

Silly Meagan. When will you learn to get out of God's way? Just get out of the way! Get out of your own way!

What Next, Lord?

Meagan E. Ahlstrom

You know, for the longest time I have held a very special place in my heart for pretty much the whole year of 2007. What an amazingly eventful year. [Some personal achievements removed], I saw Billy Joel front row and center! I saw Celine Dion LIVE! I went to Vegas. I drove across the country with one of my best friends. I went to L.A. And I started working for Estée Lauder again! Phew! That's quite a list, right? And on top of that, my niece Olive was born! Woo-hoo '07!

Problem is, after such an incredible year, I have been somewhat hating on '08 just because it hasn't been as eventful. Or at least it hasn't felt like it. Until now…

I turned in my notice yesterday. I can't believe I actually did it! I turned in my two weeks' notice. I am officially moving to Chicago. After I did it yesterday, it just hit me how eventful this year really has been. Sure, I've been in the same place. And sure, I haven't traveled near as much. But I have worked very hard at a job I love and gained experience and knowledge that will only take me farther and to the next level professionally.

In addition, I have learned that I have my own life. I am busy, successful, and it's satisfying. And it's not because of anyone. It's outside of everyone. I have my own life! Here I am, a little older, a little wiser, and definitely a little more me!

Set My Mind on Things Above

Meagan E. Ahlstrom

Lord, I want "God things." I want to be a Proverbs 31 woman! Give me strength, Lord. Forgive me, for my sins, for ignoring Your Word, and for believing that I knew what was best for me.

Make all sin disgusting in my eyes. Fill my heart with heavy conviction if I'm ever tempted to slip.

You know my heart, Lord. And I want to live the desires of my heart! I want to live what my heart knows! Help me, Jesus. Please!

I want to find and know my identity in You, and not live searching for reassurance and praise due to my random feelings of unworthiness. Show me who I am in You, Lord. I am seeking Your face so that You can show me and I can know. Set my mind on things above, Lord. Set my mind on things above!

Colossians 3:1-2: "Since, then, you have been raised with Christ, set your hearts on things above, where Christ is, seated at the right hand of God. Set your minds on things above, not on earthly things."

Don't Let "Me" Get in the Way

Meagan E. Ahlstrom

Lord, if there is one thing I know I can do well, it's dream big. My devotional today is about taking the initiative against daydreaming. Sometimes, or a lot of the time, I tend to get so caught up dreaming about how I want things to be that I don't actually take action. I don't want to live my life that way, Father. I know You have given me a heart that dreams big, and I know You want those dreams for my life. (Well, at least the ones that line up with Your will, of course.) But I also know that the dreams You Yourself have for my life are MORE than I could imagine.

Lord, I want Your will for my life. I want Your heart, Your plan, and the future You hold for me. I know You are doing a new thing in my life, and I want it! I am excited about it, though it can be very hard at times. Sometimes I am so blinded by my feelings that I can't see straight…but not tonight. Thank You for keeping me strong. Amen!

I know this is a new thing You are working in me, Father, and I don't want to mess it up. Lord, I don't want to get in my own way. Please, Jesus, help me from getting in my own way.

Keep me strong. Keep me focused. Help me become more disciplined in the time I spend with You and in finding time to spend with You. Help me get my priorities straight, Father, please! I want to spend good, in-depth, real quality time with You. I enjoy it! But I don't do it regularly enough or for a long enough period of time. But Lord, I want to meet You. I want to meet You. I want Your will for my life, Lord. Please!

Keep me strong. I do NOT want to fall into temptation. So, Lord, help me remain strong so I don't get distracted. I don't want to allow anything to keep me from this new thing, Father. And I don't want to get in the way of whatever You are working on.

Ephesians 1:18-19

I pray that the eyes of your heart may be enlightened in order that you may know the hope to which He has called you, the riches of His glorious inheritance in His holy people, and His incomparable great power for us who believe.

50 and 30…It's Just that Simple!

Rebecca L. Ahlstrom

Each birthday for me comes with a sting since the tragedy. Knowing I asked Meagan to drive, so we switched seats two minutes before the collision, and she was in the very seat I had been in for eight hours prior. She was "taken." I was left. STING.

Now the spiritual side of me, which is strong by HIS grace, knows GOD IS GOD and although He could have prevented her death, He chose not to. In fact, He chose to give her LIFE!

On the flip side, my very human heart struggles every day with the crash and the outcome. And although days seem to just roll into each other, birthdays are especially painful—mine AND hers.

Today, November 28, I turned 50. For years I actually dreaded this day because Meagan and Melody used to talk about throwing me a 50th birthday party, and if you know them—well, enough said. But today went by quietly, and that's how I needed it to be. All day when someone would wish me "Happy Birthday," I would say, "It's our 30th anniversary too, and we are focusing on that." Thirty years with Leo—crazy, trying, good times! He is my true soul mate!

Now as I sit here tonight, I feel a stirring in my heart. The same God who spared me at birth has decided to give me 50 years of life. Not LIFE like Meagan is experiencing, but still life and a chance to share His redeeming grace. So although I woke up with a very sad and heavy soul, I want to close my day declaring a thankful heart.

I am thankful for My Leo, who still desires to come home to me every day. Thankful for my children, Aaron, Meagan, and Melody, and that God gave me the honor of being their mother. Thankful that I still have my mom and dad and that they never gave up on me!!

Thankful for my sisters and their families who I love. Thankful for the host of friends the Lord has put in my life—friends who love me, hold me up, and encourage me even when I have nothing to give in return. And SOOO thankful to My God, who has not loosened His grip on me!!!!

It is quite overwhelming to see how my life has changed! Quite overwhelming to see the outpouring of love from so very many during this time!! Quite overwhelming to be held up and carried by the Body of Christ. I feel like each message, birthday wish, and card is a drop of spiritual rain on my aching soul. So…I am thankful for the rain!!

50 and 30…today, I am thankful. Today, it's just that simple.

Psalm 32:7

You are my hiding place;
  You will protect me from trouble
  and surround me with songs of deliverance.

You Surround Me

Meagan E. Ahlstrom

You surround me.
In all I do you are with me.
You are in my thoughts,
For I think of you all the time.
You are in my dreams,
For even when I sleep I need you with me.
You are in my prayers,
For I find comfort in knowing
You are with me—always!
You are in my heart,
For you are the one I love.
You are my love.
You surround me.

The Full Meagan Elaine Ahlstrom

Meagan E. Ahlstrom

I don't want to move without You, Lord. I am in a place…I am just realizing there is no way to go but "Your" way. I want Your will for my life. I believe anything less will leave me miserable and unsatisfied. And that is no way to live, Lord. No way to live.

I miss feeling like I know what I am supposed to be doing. I miss being a part of something—participating in something that is real. I can't even remember the last time I felt that way, but I know I will never have those feelings without You.

Are you excited? Are you excited, Lord, that I am getting it? That I am starting to see it? Starting to see that there is more than me. There is more in this world; there is more for my life than just me.

I want to find it, Lord. I want to be sure. I want to know. I want to know what to do. I want to be the whole me. The complete me. The full MEAGAN ELAINE AHLSTROM You created me to be—right now—in this place—in this year.

Show me, Lord. I won't move until You do. I am not going to move until You show me.

Psalm 9:9-10

The Lord is a refuge for the oppressed,
    a stronghold in times of trouble.

Those who know Your name will trust in You,
    for You, Lord, have never forsaken those who seek You.

Let Me In, Lord

Rebecca L. Ahlstrom

Lord, I am angry. I am angry with You. I confess this in fear and humility because I know You don't owe me anything and I deserve nothing. But I had a relationship with You. I depended on You. And You could have prevented this tragedy, but You chose not to. My family is falling apart, and it seems You are just letting it happen.

What is the point of praying if You are going to let things happen as they come? What is the point of believing and having faith if You let us destroy each other by our free wills? What is the point of it all if destruction can fall on us like the unjust?

I am angry for what this tragedy has done to my faith and to my relationship with You. I am angry that I don't even know what I believe or how to pray. I am angry that I am expected to go on with life—be joyful, forgiving, and as though I have not been crippled.

I MISS MY DAUGHTER! I MISS MEAGAN!! I have no one else like her! A huge part of me died in that car with her! I don't know how to do this. People keep talking. People are praying. But I feel like a stranger on a city sidewalk being knocked around without direction. I do not know how to do life without her!

Days roll into each other. Life is a painful blur. Each day brings a night. Each night brings a morning. And I am deeply sad. I am deeply wounded.

Yet…even in the darkness I cannot turn from You. Even when I feel hopeless, I cannot turn from You. Because You are my salvation. You are my God. I have to believe You will bring redemption. I have to believe You will cause "good" to come from this because Your Word says it. I have to believe there is a bigger picture, for I know Your ways are not my ways and Your thoughts are higher than my thoughts.

Let me in, Lord. Let me in. Give me a glimpse of Your heart. Regardless of the condition of mine, please don't let go of Your grip on me! Keep your promises, Lord, even when I grieve You.

Psalm 62:1-2

Truly my soul finds rest in God;
   my salvation comes from Him.

Truly He is my rock and my salvation;
   He is my fortress, I will never be shaken.

You and Me

Meagan E. Ahlstrom

Lord, I want to be like Peter in John chapter 21. I want to be overwhelmed with my realization of how much I love You. I want to love You far more than anything in heaven and anyone on Earth. And although You are far more important to me than anything that was and anything that ever will be, just how much of my life reflects my love for You? So much of my energy is put into worrying about situations that are totally out of my hands and fussing over pain that I ultimately caused myself.

I want Your presence to be what matters most. I want Your words to be the ones I long to hear and hold onto the tightest. I want Your opinion of me and plan for my life to be the only one that matters.

I miss You, Jesus. And I know I'm the one that hasn't been making the effort. Forgive me for not meeting You. For not spending more time with You. You are worthy of so much more! So much more than I can ever give.

May it just be us for as long as You need. What is greater in life than spending my days with You? Serving You? I will try so much harder to make You the focal point of my life! Again, Lord, forgive me. I love You!

Give Me Your Eyes, Lord

Meagan E. Ahlstrom

Lord, there is still a lot of junk in my heart that I need You to help me clear out. I don't want to get in the way of anyone pressing into You. I don't want to let the enemy use me as a tool in his schemes.

Give me Your eyes, Lord, to see the traps of the enemy. And give me Your heart, Lord, so I can do not only what is best for others, but what is best for me. Help me, Lord. I do not want to live even an ounce of my old life.

I know You have called me to great things. I think we are on the same page there, Lord—I just have to get my steps right.

I only want You, Jesus. I only want You. Consume me, Lord. I want to be every ounce of what You want me to be. And Lord, please take care of tomorrow. And, as for yesterday…what's the point of looking back, unless of course, I learn from it.

The Countdown Begins

Meagan E. Ahlstrom

It's Monday, and I have the day off. It's been a very nice, relaxing day. I feel so at peace. What a remarkable feeling this whole situation brings. I know that I keep using that word, but it truly is remarkable.

Now that I have put in my notice and am openly talking about it (there are still quite a few people who don't know yet), it seems that every conversation I have with others is about this move!

…

It is amazing being so "aware" of this pivotal point in my life that will completely change the outcome of my future. Well, actually, my future will be exactly what it is supposed to be since I am so certain that Chicago is my "next step," but choosing to take it—that is why it is a change.

I could easily stay here in Nashville and live this life, and it would be good. But I have chosen to listen, to obey, to TRUST, and to MOVE! I am so excited, Lord! The countdown begins!

And for old time's sake…Grace, grace, Father! May I see what You can do! I love You with my whole heart, Lord! I love You! Thank You for speaking so clearly and RIGHT to me!

5,300,000 Forgiven

Meagan E. Ahlstrom

I was really thinking the other day about all the sins that I have committed and all the sins I will commit. Did you know, and I am guessing, that by the time I am 85 years old (if I live that long), I will have committed 5,300,000 sins! Can you believe that! That's like 15 or 20 sins a day. And on Judgment Day, when I stand before God and I have to account for every sin that I have committed, Jesus will grab my hand and say, "Father, this one's with Me!" Oh, it gives me chills. And then my blessed Father is going to smile and let the "5,300,000 sins in 85 years" girl enter heaven!

It makes my eyes water every time I think about it. He is such a merciful God! And oh, how I love Him. To think that every time I sincerely and truly ask for forgiveness, the Lord of Lords, my Daddy God, forgives me and then forgets about it.

Psalm 103:11-12

For as high as the heavens are above the earth,
   so great is His love for those who fear Him;

as far as the east is from the west,
   so far has He removed our transgressions from us.

Airport Joe

Rebecca L. Ahlstrom

I've been saying in faith, "I forgive," since a few days after the crash. A couple of years later, God used a simple situation to reveal the condition of my heart.

As our church team began our journey home from a mission's trip to the Czech Republic, I offered a very elderly gentleman the seat next to me on the crowded bus to the Prague airport. The grey-haired gentleman was a kind soul who spoke in broken English. I, of course, speak zero Czech. Forced into very close quarters, awkwardly squished in a space meant for one, we managed to dialogue.

At the end of our ride, in an effort to remember this pleasant encounter and gentle conversation, I asked him his name. He gave me a warm smile and said, "My name is Joe." Time stopped. The oxygen seemed to vanish inside the bus while my mind flashed back to the day of the tragedy. I couldn't breathe. I felt like someone was sitting on my chest!

A few moments that seemed like minutes passed. I captured my runaway thoughts, took a deep breath, and finally returned his smile. I wondered what he thought about my delay. But I had an awakening! This was God checking my heart. Or better yet, God was letting me see my heart's condition in real time!

You see, the "other driver" that crashed into our lives in 2009…his name is also Joe, and I had not been able to speak his name because of the pain it caused me.

But I knew in my soul I had forgiven him from the beginning—before he ever asked, never knowing if he would ever ask. I knew my faith demanded that I forgive him as Christ had forgiven me. And this moment, this encounter in Prague was my confirmation. I can declare that I knew in that instant that my heart had indeed forgiven. And ONLY GOD can move on a messed-up heart like mine!

If I could have found a "symbolic rock" to take home like many others from the mission's trip for this moment of revelation, I would have. But a photo with Joe from Prague would have to do.

I grabbed a church friend, and we chased Joe down in the airport parking lot to get a photo of the two of us. As we approached him, he smiled as I took his hand and said, "Hello, Joe. My name is Rebecca. And I want to thank you for giving me such a gift."

1 Corinthians 4:4-5

My conscience is clear, but that does not make me innocent. It is the Lord who judges me. Therefore judge nothing before the appointed time; wait until the Lord comes. He will bring to light what is hidden in darkness and will expose the motives of the heart. At that time each will receive their praise from God.

What More Is There?

Meagan E. Ahlstrom

My "Utmost for His Highest" for today, March 3rd, is spot on! It is truly remarkable how many times I may read these passages and devotionals, and yet God uses them in such different ways each time. And sometimes, it is as if God is speaking directly to me through them. It is truly inspiring. For instance, today's devotional says, "Pour yourself out. Don't testify about how much you love Me and don't talk about the wonderful revelations you have had, just 'Feed My Sheep!'"

Basically, it is talking about The Great Commission, God's call for our lives. How we are to be obedient to that calling and spread His gospel. This is what concerns Him most, not how much we cry out that we love Him, etc.

And look at it! Look at just my last entry! It's as if just like that, in a matter of hours, God has not only heard me—of course—but He has answered me.

He doesn't want me to just start filling the majority of my days with thoughts of Him so I can prove He means more to me than others, or so I can feel better and have some relief of this pain inside. No, it is so much more than that. It is not just about my relationship with Him and how I feel and what I want. Even though I am so heartsick at times, that is truly the extent of my worries.

I can still feel peace, and I still have hope, and I know God has a plan for me. And I find great comfort in that, even if I do not know what that plan is. And I can find comfort in it since I know to some extent—though I may never know fully—the surpassing love of God. To think, there are people right now hurting for very severe reasons, crying out to God for help and understanding and strength and clarity. And worse—there are people right now hurting for very severe reasons who do not even know the love of God or have any hope or even one moment's peace.

And not to discredit any pain I may feel in my life, but at least I have God. At least I know His love and have Him in my life, and really…what more is there?

Meet My Friend?

Meagan E. Ahlstrom

Lord, would You meet my friend? Meet him all throughout his day. Allow him to see You. Keep him up at night. Let him see You.

Soften his heart, Lord. Soften his heart towards others. Show him how to break down those walls. Show him how to live free! Free from all pain, all doubt, all suffering. I know no one can do this but You, Lord. No one can help him but You, Lord. Please! Help him. Bring him joy. Unexplainable joy that is only from You. That he cannot explain. May he catch himself just laughing at the simplest things, Lord.

May he wake up tomorrow in a great mood. May all sickness be gone, in Your name. And may he wake up healed, feeling refreshed and joyful. Bring Him peace, Father, please. Overwhelming peace. I rebuke all depression. ALL depression, all self-doubt, all worrying. May he only see You, Lord.

Please, Father God, may he only see You! Bring peace and joy, and may he only see You! Lord, please, be with him.

Amen! Amen! Amen!

Wash Your Feet?

Meagan E. Ahlstrom

Yesterday's devotional in "My Utmost for His Highest" was wonderful. I read it right before I went to bed. I didn't journal yesterday because I was really down and felt a little lost. Sometimes I am a little overwhelmed with feelings of "what am I doing here?" and "I could be doing something so much better." Then, I read "My Utmost," and it was perfect! Exactly what I needed to hear! I almost wrote about how perfect it was, but it was so late.

The devotional was about how we must be willing to let go. It says, "When you have no vision from God, no enthusiasm left in your life, and no one watching and encouraging you, it requires the grace of Almighty God to take the next step in your devotion to Him, in reading and studying of His Word, in your family life or in your duty to Him."

So amazing! I worked all day yesterday and just felt washed! I was so overwhelmed with feelings of confusion and frustration. Some days I can see exactly what I want and where I want to be, and other days I feel as if I am going nowhere or just wasting my time! What a mess!

And then, just like that—I am reminded it is not about what I want or where I want to go. It is about God's vision for my life. It is about serving God in all I do, even if it is a job that is possibly temporary. And I will only find peace and see things clearly and have a vision for my life when I am seeking God.

How can He show me what He has planned for me if I am not seeking Him or listening for His voice?

It continues, "We lose interest and give up when we have no vision, no encouragement, and no improvement, but only experience our everyday life with its trivial tasks. The thing that really testifies for God and for the people of God in the long run is steady perseverance, even when the work cannot be seen by others. And the only way to live an undefeated life is to live looking to God."

Amazing! It is so true for me! When I lose motivation, all of my day feels like a bunch of meaningless, trivial tasks, which makes for a very tough day for me. I want every single day of my life to matter—not to me, but for the kingdom of God.

It finishes by saying, "Never allow yourself to think that some tasks are beneath your dignity or too insignificant for you to do, and remind yourself of the example of Christ in John 13:1-17."

Yesterday, I allowed myself to feel very discouraged about the pay cut I took when accepting this job. I even complained to a co-worker but felt sick to my stomach the second I did because I knew it was wrong of me. And God drove the point home through yesterday's devotional. Fantastic! Again, He makes Himself so very evident.

I love You, Lord. Thank You for everything—just because You are a great God! I love You! Amen!

I Cannot Pretend Anymore

Meagan E. Ahlstrom

What a crazy time this is for me. God is seriously testing my faith right now and teaching me how to be patient and really trust Him.

I really need to get some things straight. I cannot pretend I'm something I'm not anymore.

It's the Word of God, Meagan!

Meagan E. Ahlstrom

Oh Lord, I don't read the Bible anymore.

I do my devotionals in Max Lucado's "3:16," and I am currently reading "The Papa Prayer," but I don't read the Bible. I read everything ABOUT the Bible. I just don't read the Bible. I hate to even admit it, but I can't deny it any longer.

I started crying tonight as I read through a particular paragraph in "The Papa Prayer." I started crying when it hit me…I don't pick up the Bible anymore. Why is this? I realized, or so it seems, that it's because every person who has ever deeply hurt me has been a Christian. I suppose I expect things to be different from fellow believers. Anyway, why would I want to read and study what they do—even if I DO believe every word in it?

But it's really not about anyone else. It's about ME. I am very aware that it is ME. It is the anger that I allow to build in my heart that leads me to feel this way about the Word of God. It's the WORD OF GOD, MEAGAN! And yet, I let myself get so worked up by everyone else and how they may or may not have treated me to the point where it affects me on a spiritual level. And all I can really think is, "Good play, Satan!"

But Lord, I am bigger than that. More so, You living in me is much, much bigger than that!

Father, please heal my heart. I don't want to hurt anymore. I don't want to take this anger out on You anymore…or on me. I am hurting inside, and I don't want to just numb the pain by forgetting about it or hiding it behind other things. I want to be healed. Please, Father, heal my heart of this pain, this insecurity, this anger. Take it all from me, Lord. It has nothing to do with You. And I don't want things living in my heart if they have nothing to do with You.

I love You, Lord. That's the only thing I want to live in my heart—my complete, undeniable, unrelenting love for You!

Amen! Amen! Amen!

Psalm 116:1-2

I love the Lord, for He heard my voice,
  He heard my cry for mercy.

Because He turned His ear to me,
  I will call on Him as long as I live.

I Love You Still!

Rebecca L. Ahlstrom

I am going to **SIERRA LEONE, AFRICA**! *Seventeen months waiting, and in one day Leo got me in on a mission's trip through our church with four women, led by our women's director. God, You have made a way for me to literally walk in Meagan's shoes!*

I have been warned about the darkness there. There is no electricity, only gas generators on for a few hours every night. My fear of darkness is so intense since the crash, and this is the only thing that feeds severe anxiety about the journey. I will be without Leo for the first time, but I know You are with me. I am going to a foreign land, but what do I have to fear after everything I have been through? Being trapped in darkness is my biggest enemy. Yet You will keep me...I must believe this!

***

We flew into Freetown's Lungi International Airport and could barely see it for the lack of lights. After landing, we were ushered out by our host church toward the ferry, no questions asked. I couldn't breathe. Only a few random lights on the double-decker boat, and I literally could not discern water from sky. I have never witnessed such blackness! I remember telling myself repeatedly, "Breathe." I trusted our leaders as to our destination. I did not fear a tragedy, only living through one again.

With standing room only on the ferry, I made my way to Santa, the pastor's wife, who was leading us with such confidence and grace—her entourage close by. People knew her! She was well-respected.

She drew me in. If you could see her beautiful, warm eyes! She knew my name, but until I shared "who I was," she did not connect the dots. She exclaimed, "Oh my. You're her mother! We've prayed for you!" The overwhelming darkness faded a little as I began to explain how Meagan had joined the mission's team headed to Sierra Leone 17 months prior but the tragedy abruptly ended her plans. Then You, God, made a way so I could be there literally in Meagan's shoes! I was a willing vessel, open to whatever You had planned for me. I cried because I felt purpose in being there. PURPOSE!

As I stood closely, Santa began to speak truth to me. She reminded me that though we face troubles, You are ever near, totally in control, and that You did not abandon Meagan or me!

As we continued to talk and the ferry moved ever so slowly to its port, in a beautiful strong accent, she asked me, "But can you say you love Him still?" I cried and shared how wounded and confused I was. She asked me again, "But can you say you love Him still?" Inadvertently, I responded from my aching soul of how I agonized over my daughter. She let me talk for a few minutes as I cried, and she comforted me. Yet once again she leaned in and asked, "But can you say you love Him still?" After moments of silence and a flood of tears, I finally responded, "Yes."

A day or two later, we were based in Bo for about a week visiting villages deep in the bush, loving on children in orphanages and schools, touring the medical facility and kicking up some dirt in the soon-to-be local college—all while in Meagan's shoes. Sunday, however, we were guests at the main church in Bo, clothed in our African-bought dresses.

The sounds of prayer and singing could be heard from the street. The nursery was on the front porch, where the breeze wasn't hindered by the walls of a building. Once inside, a part of me felt an overwhelming calm, like being home. My soul was excited by the most brilliant array of colors through the congregation; the women dressed in traditional attire and headdress! I thought, "These people aren't afraid of color!"

As we were escorted to the front pews, I saw a beautiful young lady that looked just like Meagan. She was stunning! Over the singing, I signed, "You are beautiful!" and with my hand over my heart, I added, "You look like my daughter!" then motioned that I wanted a headdress like hers. Her smile captivated me. We locked eyes for a long time as our group walked forward. I mean, danced forward!

As a worshipper, I was immediately caught up with the congregation in the music and didn't want it to end. It didn't matter to me that they were singing in other languages, because occasionally I would catch the name of Jesus and my spirit leaped with more excitement! Pastor Shodankeh's message was a mixture of English and Krio from what I remember, trying to appease both "the Americans" and his people.

I soaked in his passionate deliverance of the Gospel, unaware of the increasing extreme heat or my melting body. I was mesmerized by the people, their passion, their display of color, their love! I wanted my family to be there so badly, to join me so I didn't have to leave. Then what I thought was the close of the service was actually Pastor coming to invite me to share my story. I almost crumbled in complete humility. Could this be happening? Did You make a way for me to not only be in Sierra Leone in Meagan's place, in Meagan's shoes, but also have a platform to tell my story and share my Meagan?! Oh, Father, You have heard my heart! You have seen my tears!

I walked up to the platform and shared how comfortable I felt in the midst of the congregation, as Pastor Shodankeh interpreted for me. Santa stood behind me with her hand on my back. Two greatly anointed Kingdom-priests were near me, such presence of the Holy Spirit that I could barely stand. I shared our story briefly. I remember saying that I didn't have to explain this pain in my heart because I was with a people that knew suffering, knew tragedy and devastation, knew the pain of loss, BUT also knew the grace of God that carried us when we could hold on no longer! The people were crying. They knew! I didn't have to say much. They knew! I affirmed that our

Meagan is experiencing the ultimate life because she is now with the One she adored since she was a little girl. Then I shared my God-encounter with Santa on the ferry and how she asked me three times if I could say, "I love Him still," and on the third time, I said, "Yes." But I realized that I never actually said it!

So I stood among the congregation in Your presence and said, "I declare before you today that I love the Lord still. For the first time in 17 months, I LOVE YOU, LORD!" They applauded, cried, and prayed over me! So many hugs and encouragement in other tribal languages. So many tears. "PURPOSE," like I had prayed. I whispered, "Take me now, Father, please! There is nothing that could surpass this!"

I was told later that my testimony had challenged others who struggled with similar issues. They went home, got on their knees, and said, "If Re-becca can do it, then so can I. I love You, Lord." Oh, Father!! What goodness You have shown me through my brokenness!! My Sovereign Lord, Thou art with me. I know You are. If it were not so, I would not have this joy I've found in this broken but blessed country of Sierra Leone.

During our last night in Bo, Pastor Shodankeh and Santa hosted an outside worship service as a send-off. High on a hill, the church congregation and townspeople gathered. Before I knew it, there was a huge crowd and the night had become so eerily dark. Pastor began calling out various people to sing; some were hesitant, others flowing in their anointing. Then I began to tremble realizing Santa was right! She had previously challenged me, "Leave everything you can...here! Leave everything here, Re-becca!" So, I quietly made my way to her and whispered the unction I felt on my heart. I could hear Meagan saying, "Sing, Mom!"

Santa walked over to Pastor Shodankeh and whispered what I shared. Soon after, he waved me over. I told the crowd I was stepping way out of my comfort zone and for the first time ever I was going to sing a worship song—a song I found that our daughter wrote a couple of months before the tragedy.

I had never sung in public before, but I would that night! I was determined to declare the glory of the Lord, and as I sang to Him, I envisioned Meagan also singing before His throne.

It wasn't about how good I sounded but more importantly about shaking off some chains that had me imprisoned. It was about standing in the pitch blackness of night—fearless—looking up to the velvet skies and surrendering everything I could to my Father.

From the top of a hill, I left a part of me there as I sang Meagan's song through tears:

(chorus)

"Thank You, Lord, for all that You have done.
And thank You, Lord, for who I have become.
In everything You do,
I'm gonna thank You,
Lord, thank You with praise."

GO, GOD! GO, MEAGAN!!

Psalm 37:5-6
"Commit your way to the Lord;
* trust in him and he will do this:*

He will make your righteousness shine like the dawn;
* the justice of your cause like the noonday sun."*
(NIV (Zondervan))

Isaiah 26:9

My soul yearns for You in the night;
  in the morning, my spirit longs for You.

Anyone

Meagan E. Ahlstrom

Anyone
They say they can see it in my eyes and that it's all over my face.
Understandable...for you are not just "anyone."

Someone
They ask what someone could put such a smile on my face.
No answer...for you are far from being "someone."

Everyone
They wonder why I keep you so secret. "Why not tell the world?"
Sacred...and all will be known in due time.

Anywhere
They say not to get so attached, for my true love could be anywhere.
Ridiculous...anywhere? I know exactly where you are, for my heart is with you.

Somewhere
They ask who you are and where you are. "Do we even know who he is?"
Crazy...they don't see you, but you are always somewhere with me.

Everywhere
They wonder how I can be so happy when all I appear to be is alone.
Alone? ... Can they really not see that you are everywhere?

Anything
Maybe I don't know you—completely.
But that doesn't stop me from wanting to do anything for you.

Something
Maybe we haven't officially met.
But even that doesn't seem to stop this "something" I feel for you.

Everything
Maybe

That Simple Truth

Meagan E. Ahlstrom

Lord, I need Your help. I need Your guidance.

I know I don't spend as much time with You as I should and now obviously as I need. Forgive me for all the times I try to walk this life alone and for not seeking You constantly along the way. I am aware that the only time I seem to call out Your name and *truly* seek Your face is when I am in trouble or my heart is aching.

When will I realize that if I would ask You to walk with me all day and seek Your face even in the good times, my heart would not ache as much in the bad times as it does now?! When will that simple "truth" be set in my soul?

The Search

Meagan E. Ahlstrom

Love is truly an amazing thing. What is it in us that desires so much to find a companion? To find someone we connect with on such an intense level? And why must we seek that out, or why do we try to seek that out in one person?

I believe you can learn from every person you meet. Every person can teach you something or help you grow in some way—even if it is simply what not to do.

Why is it that we need that physical, mental, emotional, and spiritual connection with just one human being? And is our "search" for that one person what truly causes our relationship downfall with others? Because in our search to find that "one," we place that pressure and expectation on everyone we meet until we meet the "one." Or is there even a "one"?

What if our desire and heart's longing to find such a personal and rare connection with another human being is really our heart's cry for a true relationship with our heavenly Father? Our Father being the ONLY "one" who can truly and fully meet that expectation without ever letting us down or hurting us. Maybe rather than being drawn to those Godly characteristics within each other, we are really being drawn to God Himself.

Only God can truly satisfy that thirst, making us strong from the inside out. Giving us an inner peace, a confidence and a sense of self-worth because of how He sees us, how

He's made us, and how He loves us. And unlike man, God cannot let us down, leave us or, love us less.

Once we realize who we are in Christ, we will always have that identity. We will always be what He has made us to be and called us to be as long as we feed that relationship and strengthen it. Only then will we have true peace and stop "the search"...realizing that there is no search. Realizing that what we are looking for is with us right now! At this very moment!

Only You (worship song)

Meagan E. Ahlstrom

There are no problems.
There are no struggles.
There's no temptation
Or pride.

I feel nothing but
Your Holy presence.
Nothing else matters
Or exists.

Only You.
Only You.
In Your presence,
There's only You.

Only You.
Only You.
In Your presence,
There's only You.

Here's to Mine

Meagan E. Ahlstrom

People are so similar. We all laugh. We cry. We hurt. We bleed. It is so amazing, really, that with so many things in common, we seem to have such a difficult time getting along—or at least for long periods of time.

More than just basic human needs of food, water, shelter, the need to belong—we share other things in common, like the fear of change. The fear of starting a new life when we are so settled, so comfortable in the one we already have. Even if it is not a good one. Even if it is not the best life for us.

We can't see past ourselves. I believe that is why we don't like change and why we are afraid to start new things. I think that is also why, though we are so similar, we can't get along—because we can't see past ourselves.

But if, for a moment, we could. If we could find the strength to see beyond the "me" in order to change, to embark on a new journey, a new life. That would be truly amazing. That is what would make a difference. That is where we would find a difference—in ourselves, in our hearts, in the world.

The unknown. Our ability to admit that we are not in control. That there are things greater than ourselves. That many other things are more important than us, than our wants and desires. THAT knowledge, THAT awareness— that is what makes the difference. That is what makes a life!

And here's to mine…a soon-to-be, long-awaited, new beginning.

Why Do I Still Fight You?

Meagan E. Ahlstrom

Lord, I carry a heavy load of baggage.

I know, Father, that You don't want me to carry such a burden, and I know that You want me to lay all my burdens down at Your feet. But Lord, for some reason I am hanging on. Help me put the past behind me. Help me lay down my worries and find peace in You and only You. Help me not take the past out on others but lay it down so it is no longer even an issue in my life.

Father, I need You. Please, bring peace to my heart. Help me to allow You in. Help me find my security in You and only You and no longer put such heavy expectations on others. I know that only You can fill this hole in my heart. I don't know why I still fight You.

Psalm 4:6-8

Let the light of Your face shine on us.

Fill my heart with joy
   when their grain and new wine abound.

In peace I will lie down and sleep,
   for You alone, Lord,
   make me dwell in safety.

Her Mother Teresa

Rebecca L. Ahlstrom

When Leo (and I) accepted the job offer in the Chicago area, it was a major turning point in our lives. We were leaving Aaron and Meagan for the first time EVER and separating them from our youngest, Melody, who was only 15 and moving with us. We were leaving our house, our "Nashville home" and friends of 20+ years, and I was leaving an incredible job. During all of this emotional processing, Melody's Airedale Terrier, Gracey, began to spiral down from Addison's disease, which she had battled for four years. And I struggled spiritually…surely God would not let her die…not when we were giving up so much for "the call." My mind just would not accept it. We fought for a miracle.

Leo moved north to begin his new position as Worship Pastor; Melody and I were to join him weeks later. It was during this separation that Gracey's condition worsened. I still could not believe God would let this happen—not now. But He did. And we put her to rest and had to make the journey without her.

Years later, I began to search for a particular email that Meagan sent me during this emotional time. Her email of wisdom and insight changed everything for me—especially my perspective. I found it recently and I cried. I miss you, Meagan!

[An e-mail to me from Meagan]:

You know, my view on it is this: only God knows when and how we are going to die. NOT that Gracey deserves the pain or disease, but it must have been God's will to place her with our family, to be in such a loving house, to have such WONDERFUL doggie companions, and to live such a blessed little life, you know? It's all in His hands and it obviously has been from the start.

There are plenty of things in this world I will never understand: starving children, child molestation, animal abuse, but one thing I can TRUST is that there is a GOD who loves His children and all of His creations, and who sees and completely sees the whole BIG picture. Mother Teresa spent so much of her life faithfully serving God by helping the sick and dying. She was confident that He put her in their lives and in those places for such a purpose—to usher them through death to life. She never blamed Him, and although I am sure she faced testing times when those she served passed away, I doubt that she felt God was not being good or just.

If Gracey for some odd, unexplainable reason is to suffer from this sickness, all I can say is, "Thank You, God, for allowing us to be her Mother Teresa." [signed] Meagan

Psalm 73:26

My flesh and my heart may fail,
  but God is the strength of my heart
  and my portion forever.

The Way Out

Meagan E. Ahlstrom

When you are feeling troubled
  And all alone,
When you feel like emptiness is
  All you've ever known,
Remember…
He has also been there.

When close friends condemn you
All men doubt you,
When you feel like crying
  Is all you can do,
Remember…
He has also been there.

When you feel pain, heartache
  And despair,
When you feel hopeless and betrayed,
  Darkness in the air,
Remember…
He has also been there.

He's familiar with it all,
  Bore it on the cross.
Stretched out His arms in love,
  Paid the ultimate cost.
Remember…
He's the ONLY One that's been there!

Fruitful Life

Meagan E. Ahlstrom

I cannot believe it's already December! In a matter of days, I will have officially been here [in Chicago] for three months! In two weeks Mel will be married! I am working and truly beginning to have my own life here. And it's good. It's a good thing.

It snowed yesterday for the first "real" time. It has snowed before, but now it's up to six inches, which is a very big snow by Nashville standards. So, I am excited. It happened so fast! It will be interesting to see how I do with my first Chicago winter. I actually had to buy snow boots today for the long trek through the parking lot at work. Crazy!

On another note, I've noticed some changes in my attitude, and I believe I have pinpointed the reason for the abnormal eating/depressed feeling issue. For the past couple of weeks, I haven't been spending time in the Word. I am no longer memorizing Scripture, and I actually didn't go to church last Sunday because I was too tired from work. Actually, I had stayed up too late the night before watching a movie, and THAT made me too tired for church. That makes two Sundays I've missed since I have moved here. And yes, I'm counting. It's important to me.

What's interesting to think about is that it's late right now. I'm writing and watching a movie. It may be even later before I decide to get in bed, but guess who will get up for work in the morning and even be early? Yes…me!

I have had some very disturbing dreams lately. I have been depressed, anxious, and at times insecure. And it has finally hit me! I am casually pushing God out of my day and allowing room for so much else. So much that is not of God. Just thoughts or feelings of little peace. But I see now. I see this trap the enemy is using to trip me up, but I'm choosing to do something about it. I studied some in the Word today. I started reading "The Fruitful Life," and I'm going to definitely be at church Sunday.

When I first got here, I dove so hard into the Word of God, into strengthening my relationship with Jesus, and I immediately saw the fruit of it.

God, forgive me for losing sight of why I am here. Help me make all my time for You. There is nothing in my life without You, Lord. I want to serve You, love You, and be obedient to You always. I want to live a life that pleases You. One that reflects You.

Help me, Holy Spirit. Draw me close to You. Help me hear Your voice and follow Your promptings. Please. I love You, Jesus, with everything I am. May the choices I make, the words I speak, the life I live demonstrate that I do not find satisfaction living a life where only words represent my love for You. May it be in everything I do. In everything I am.

I love You, Lord. Forgive me, please. Keep me safe. Amen.

Proverbs 3:5-6

Trust in the Lord with all your heart
   and lean not on your own understanding;

in all your ways submit to Him,
   and He will make your paths straight.

Christmas Shoes

Rebecca L. Ahlstrom

Leo and I were not going to "do" Christmas the first year after the tragedy. There was nothing in us that wanted to put up Christmas lights or a tree. Our hearts were just too heavy. Then we remembered the previous December when Leo, Meagan, and I returned to Illinois after hosting Melody's wedding in Nashville. We were so exhausted and thought we would forgo decorations, but Meagan wouldn't tolerate that attitude and put up our tree and lights as a surprise! Her words of proclamation that last year, with her fist lifted high, rang in our hearts: "There WILL be Christmas!!" Her face beamed with joy as she saw our response. She was so pleased!

So, in that spirit of Christmas to honor Meagan the first year of her absence, I put up our Christmas tree as family arrived from out of town. Tearfully but lovingly, I placed each ornament and strand of lights until finally the tree was decorated. In the middle of the night, the base cracked and the tree crashed into the wall. Not much was said. We just left it there…it seemed so symbolic of our lives at that point.

The second Christmas seemed harder than the first. In honor of her sister, Meagan, our youngest daughter Melody gave Leo and me a collection of beautiful purple glass ornaments for our tree. Our longtime friend, Beth Ryan, sent me a perfect ornament in honor of Meagan—a tiny, classic high-heeled red pump. It is sooo Meagan. And it got me to thinking…

It was possibly a little ambitious of me, but I solicited family and friends to help me pay tribute to our Meagan for the next year's Christmas tree: the whole tree was to be decorated with "shoe" ornaments for Meagan. As much as Meagan LOVED four-inch heels, she also LOVED colorful sneakers, so I didn't put any limits on anyone. I expected about 25 people to respond but never dreamed so many would catch the vision.

During the year, as people would find small shoe ornaments, they would send them to me with a heartfelt note. I cry with the arrival of each new shoe ornament. I tag each shoe with name and state. I post the shoe on the Facebook Group page set up in Meagan's honor, and lastly, I post a picture of the tree when it is all done. To see the tree sprinkled with love from around the country is indescribable.

After the second year, one Christmas tree would no longer hold all of the ornaments, so we bought a huge lighted wreath.

There are over 265 miniature shoes that have been sent to us in honor of our Meagan thus far. Shoes of all sorts and shapes, each tagged with the name and location of the one who lovingly sent it. And more continue to arrive. Each shoe with its own story. Each shoe has its own connection to Meagan. Each shoe—a symbol of walking this journey with our family. Each shoe—a celebration of our daughter and the impact she had on so many.

Sometimes I just sit and stare at the tree of Christmas shoes. I remember who and why, the story behind each ornament. My eyes water. I think of how much God must love her. In my heart I have to believe He lets her see the wonder of this sight. Oh, Father, I hope You let her see!

1 Peter 1:8-9

Though you have not seen Him, you love Him; and even though you do not see Him now, you believe in Him and are filled with an inexpressible and glorious joy, for you are receiving the end result of your faith, the salvation of your souls.

Happy Birthday, Jesus!

Meagan E. Ahlstrom

Happy Birthday, Jesus! ~ Thank You for all Your wonderful blessings that I in no way deserve. Bless You for my family, my friends, and all of the puppies in my life. Lord, bless You for all You have done for me and all You continue to do—for me and my family.

God, thank You, Father, for allowing me to serve You through Jesus so that I might live with You forever. Bless You, Lord, for loving me. I will thank You for that every day of my life and all through eternity—and it still won't express my gratitude completely.

I love You, Lord. I love You. Thank You for choosing me. Thank You for saving me. Thank You for blessing me. Thank You for loving me!

Happy Birthday, My Lord!

I've Stopped Counting

Meagan E. Ahlstrom

Day by day, life is getting easier. For instance, I've stopped "counting," and I officially have a job. Praise God! I start next week, and it's a fantastic opportunity with Lauder, so I am very excited. Plus, I was accepted to ECC, of course. Classes start in a couple of months, and I couldn't be happier.

It's funny how now that things are coming together, I can look back and see how little time has passed. Before, it was killing me that it has been over two months since I moved here! And now I think, "Wow. It's only been two months." I suppose it is true—everything takes time and happens in its own time.

The passing of time really can be one of the most therapeutic things, depending on where we are in our lives, I suppose. For instance, when things are great and we are truly happy, we want time to slow down. To stop! So we can cherish every moment. Then there are other times in life where we find ourselves struggling through something, and we think time can't pass quickly enough.

That's where I find myself. In a place where I just need time to pass. I want to hurry up and make it through the holidays already. I want six months to pass. A year! So that I can find myself in a new life—not just starting one.

I want to be in a new life where I don't think of certain people and certain things. And though I am no longer counting, I do still find myself crying. I am watching an old life die away and have no real time to mourn it, as I am already being forced into a new life. I did choose this new life; or at least I chose to be here and follow God's leading. But I am learning that living this life requires the sacrifice of another. And it is hard. And it is a daily struggle, but I realize I cannot have both worlds. That is why I am still crying. I have to keep reminding myself that things were never really what they were in my head.

It's as if I am mourning something that was never there. Holding onto something that only caused me pain. And that, as well, makes me cry. It's tough when you do all you can, give all you can, and try with all your might, and it's still not good enough.

I hope that my tears are truly the result of a badly bruised ego more than tears pouring over nothing and me acting like a fool.

I know better. I know I know better. I am just learning that even though I KNOW it, that doesn't mean I don't have to remind myself of it every day. Every—single—day.

Thank You (worship song)

Meagan E. Ahlstrom

Sometimes I don't know if I should stand up
And shout out Your name
Or fall down on my knees
And bury my face.
But up or down,
In or out,
No matter what the way,
I'm gonna thank You,
Lord, thank You with praise.

Thank You, Lord,
For all that You have done.
And thank You, Lord,
For who I have become.

In everything You do,
I wanna thank You,
Lord, thank You with praise.

Psalm 28:7-8

The Lord is my strength and my shield;
  my heart trusts in Him, and I am helped.

My heart leaps for joy
  and I will give thanks to Him in song.

"UNCLE!"

Rebecca L. Ahlstrom

I attended a silent retreat recently. Of about thirty women, I knew only three. The setting was a regal seminary/university nestled around a frozen lake in the middle of nowhere, Illinois, complete with beautifully crafted buildings decorated with intricate brickwork and tall stately columns. We were in a glorious winter wonderland with nature at her best.

The purpose of the retreat was to be quiet and alone with God. It wasn't time to make new friends, though that's always nice. It wasn't time to focus on women's issues, though there is a time for that. This retreat was designed specifically and strategically around being before God—one on one; communing with our Creator without holding back, and then being quiet and seeking His voice and His response; praising and listening; repenting and receiving; relenting and believing. I was 100% in!

We met in a dimly lit meeting room with very high ceilings, a long wall of ceiling-to-floor windows, a homemade life-sized wooden cross, dozens of candles, classic creaky wooden floors, and women like me wanting more of a personal God.

The focus of one of the meditation sessions was on being "thankful." It is easy to rattle off things we are all thankful for, but that was not the challenge. We were to search deep within for things HE wanted us to be thankful for. "Ask and then listen." Our host shared, "be thankful IN your circumstance, not FOR your circumstance." I laid out my yoga mat on the floor while listening to a meditation facilitator talk us into that still, chaos-free, inner place of...silence of the mind and soul.

Since the crash, my thought life is very different. My mind is literally a battlefield. I began talking to the Lord in my mind about my life and revealing those hard places of my heart. And then I slowly laid it all down and let the silence overtake me. I pressed in like suggested and asked Him to show me places to be thankful. Minutes passed. I remember wishing I could stay in that silence forever. Then the stirring began.

The Lord revealed that I used to be a very thankful person beginning with the moment I awoke. Gratitude used to easily flow from my lips. In fact, I would often thank Him for the sunshine and blue skies by saying, "I'll take that as a kiss on the forehead from God!" But no longer. He revealed that though I was thankful, I was no longer a thankful person. The crash changed me in many ways, but He challenged me against having a hardened heart.

Then He gave me a revelation I NEVER thought about. A divine, humbling, soul-wrenching thought: He said, "I pray for you. Yet you are not thankful. My Word says that I intercede daily on your behalf before the throne of my Father. Yet, are you thankful? I intercede for you because I love you, Rebecca. I want you to work on being a thankful person again. And though you feel it is impossible, if I speak it, it CAN be done."

I want a thankful heart again. I want an embracing heart. What an awakening! No doubt, mending my heart in this fashion will take some time. But I'm aware that the first painful step was asking, hearing, and accepting the revelation. God's approach reminded me of a fighting pit bull; they go right for the throat and lock their jaws; but in this case, God went right for my heart and locked His grip. And that's what I need...for Him to NEVER let go!

I cry, "UNCLE!"

We have a SAVIOR who sits at the right hand of the Father always interceding for us—One who LIVES to intercede for us! Humbling!

Thank You, Lord!!

Hebrews 7:25

Therefore, He is able to save completely those who come to God through Him, because He always lives to intercede for them.

Supernatural, Extraordinary

Meagan E. Ahlstrom

Father God, help me. Show me where to go and what to do. I want to live a supernatural, extraordinary life with You. I am so tired of the world I live in, God.

Lord, I believe that I am one of Your children and that You will use me in any way You choose. Please use me, Lord. I want to shake up the world. I want people to see You through this life I lead.

You make Yourself evident every day in my life. I want it to be evident every day to people around me that I serve You. It's not about opinions or pride. It's about why I am here, Father, on this planet! I want people to know You, God! I want people to know You, Father! And I want to know You better.

Lord, would you heal my heart of anything that does not please You? Show me where I need to straighten up. I want my life to be a blessing to You. I want to please You and honor You with every day that I live.

Lord, I am here for You. A willing vessel—with a heart for obedience. Give me guidance and favor. Speak to me. Show me where to go and which steps to take. Please, Lord, may I hear You as clearly as I did about moving here. Amen. Amen. Amen.

Just Write

Meagan E. Ahlstrom

Written in pencil on a fading Post-It note, Meagan simply wrote:

Write.
Write what you know.
Write what you don't know.
Write what you think.
Write what you feel.
Just write.

A Glimpse and She's Gone

Meagan E. Ahlstrom

Lord, forgive me for all the times I have compromised my convictions because I was too interested in what *I* wanted or what *I* thought I wanted. It's not about me. It never has been. I'm sorry, Lord. Please forgive me.

I want to change. I believe people can change for the better. I want to be disciplined. Right now I am weak; I am selfish; and not who I want to be. I see a glimpse of the woman You have called me to be; the woman I desire to be, but it's as if every time I get a glimpse of her, I destroy it by acting foolishly. That's not You. Forgive me, Lord. That's not You. And I'm sorry I have loved myself more than You at times. I am sorry I often forsake You; turn from You; and choose my will over Yours. You know my heart. I want nothing but You. Please forgive me. I love You, Father.

Romans 12:11

Never be lacking in zeal, but keep your spiritual fervor,
serving the Lord.

It's Just a Banana Shake…Or Is It?

Rebecca L. Ahlstrom

We've since defined Meagan as a "Life Coach." If you don't know Meagan in this way, here's another example.

I can recall this memory because it is forever etched in my heart (and you will see why), but I was also so impressed by her tenacity that I wrote about it when it happened in my own journal.

Meagan was an extremist, much like her father, and a few years ago she came to me and announced that she was fasting from everything but water and juice for a week (while working and going to school). Now, the reason why is not for me to say, but she was determined to excel in a private situation and believed without a doubt that God would honor her sacrifice.

I've fasted many times over the years in various forms, and so had Meagan. This was an extreme fast, and I wanted to support her.

As is normal, the first couple of days you feel you are starving! Then by the third day, your stomach has shrunk a little. But it was at the end of her sixth day that I found her curled up in a ball in her father's home studio in the dark, grasping her head in agony. I interrupted her silence and asked if I could get her something. She whispered, "No, this migraine has to pass sometime." I told her many headaches are caused by dehydration and maybe she needed liquids. She remained silent, but her body language was screaming. As her mother, I wanted to give her something for her headache, but her stomach had been empty for six days. With that thought and out of serious concern, I said, "Meagan, let me go to Sonic up the street and get you a milkshake, or better yet, a banana shake! You need something of substance, and a shake is still a liquid." Her hands began to move, she opened her eyes just enough to see me, and then she spoke with such spiritual discipline, "Who are you, Satan?!!" then mumbled, "HE will see me through this, Mom."

You know the Bible even says it's better not to make a vow to God than to make a vow and break it. And I knew this! Yet I found myself spiritually spanked by my daughter, and even more by the Holy Spirit. I realized that what I should have done knowing Meagan's determination was quietly pray for her! PRAY! How simply profound, yet it didn't cross my mind at that moment. I just wanted to feed her body and didn't think about her spirit...or her commitment.

At the end of her seven-day stretch, Meagan's persistence paid off! Not only did God honor her fast AND her attitude she kept about it, but He gave her ABOVE and BEYOND what she believed Him for. She kept her "eyes on the Author and Perfecter of her faith," even when her caring mother tried to intervene.

When you fast, FAST! Don't get distracted. And don't let the enemy, no matter what "form" he chooses to use, tempt you with foolish things, not even a banana shake.

Deuteronomy 30:11, 14

Now what I am commanding you today is not too difficult for you or beyond your reach.

No, the word is very near you; it is in your mouth and in your heart so you may obey it.

I Suffer from Something People Long For

Meagan E. Ahlstrom

I'm glancing back at the pages of this journal seeing and realizing I no longer pray for many things within. I've neglected You, God. I've neglected our relationship which has in turn neglected You.

I suffer from something people long for; something I always wanted that now controls me—I am strong. I am too strong for my own good.

I work hard and I am smart. And I am dangerously independent.

I love that I am strong—driven—confident. That I believe in myself and possess a strength that I once only dreamed of having, but I feel I have encouraged these traits too much.

Now, I am in a season where I hardly even pray. I no longer pray feeling that You are in control, but rather that I am in charge of my situation, my circumstances. So much so that I don't need to pray because I can work to reach any goal and control my emotions enough to be okay in most if not all situations.

God, You know my heart. It's not shut off or bitter. I'm not cold-hearted. I just work so hard. And as hard as I work, I still know I could work harder! I believe in working hard; in not pretending like life will bring you everything you want or need—but YOU ARE STILL GOD. YOU ARE ALWAYS GOD. And I've ignored You lately. I almost wrote that I've ignored You a little lately but even a little, even the tiniest bit, is too much!

I love You, Lord. You are the only thing good and right in my life. You are my strength, the reason I am so strong. It is Your strength that works through me. May I use it ALL for Your glory, Lord. Don't let me waver in this.

I love You!

What's the Point of All This Writing?

Meagan E. Ahlstrom

What's the point of all this writing? I mean, I know why I enjoy it—because it gives me some therapeutic emotional and spiritual release. But there has to be more to it than that. Otherwise, after finishing a journal, after it has fulfilled its purpose of being my emotional outlet, I would get rid of it. What's the point of keeping one I can no longer write in—if that's all it is for?

But no. I hang on. I keep them. To reread? To remember? And if so, are these thoughts, these moments really worth re-reading?

It's amazing how the things worth remembering—the crazy days, insane events, unbelievable stories—I never seem to write about. Like my trip to Vegas, the trek across the U.S. to Los Angeles, or even how I was in the hospital last week after being slipped a drug. But maybe it's because I know I will NEVER forget those times. And although I may not remember all the details, I will NEVER forget the actual events, the stories, the feelings.

Evident

Meagan E. Ahlstrom

There are so many things I will never understand, at least not in this life—and Lord, You never cease to amaze me! Here I was, not even an hour ago, brokenhearted, literally on my knees crying out to You. Asking for Your guidance, and then—there You are! I was on my knees with my face in the floor begging You to answer me. Begging You to take this pain from me—and the phone rings. It's my friend. He said You put it on his heart to call. We prayed.

You are beautiful, Father. I love You and will never again live a life separate from You. I do not want anything less than Your will for me. So, show me, Lord. Guide my steps and set my path. I will be obedient to Your will. Just show me.

You are everything inside of me. Everything good and right. You are my complete joy. My song. The love of my life. You are my most significant relationship. And I will do what's right by You before anything else. Let me serve You, Father. Show me the ways, all the ways I can please You, honor and bless You.

I feel such peace already. You are always so quick to make Yourself evident. And You are always evident! You are so close to me at all times. Do You remember those days long ago when I felt You were so far away? In actuality, it was just me running. How could I have not seen You?

Even now, You are so close. It's as if I can feel You holding me, whispering to me, and reminding me that You have already worked all things out according to Your good and perfect will. I trust You, Lord. I believe You. You are perfect. And I love You!

Ephesians 1:17

I keep asking that the God of our Lord Jesus Christ, the glorious Father, may give you the Spirit of wisdom and revelation, so that you may know Him better.

In the Swells

Rebecca L. Ahlstrom

Everyone is still asleep, which is a Godsend because I asked You for some quiet time last night for this morning. I wanted to get in Your Word without the distraction of anyone else, as my young family is here. Thank You for this!

Be near, Father, as I look to Your Word. Help me with this journey. Help me keep out of the way of what You are doing. Help me see past my brokenness.

First thing I opened to was one of my favorite life Scripture, Psalm 138:8 (MEV): "The Lord will fulfill His purpose for me; Your love, O Lord, endures forever—Do not forsake the work of Your hands."

I cry out to You this prayer today. I am a willing vessel. Yet I feel Your Spirit as it tugs at my heart with conviction: "Am I truly willing? How willing am I? And am I willing only if it concerns Meagan?" This stings to my core, but Lord, look deep into my heart this morning. Reveal the hidden things to me, please.

Psalm 139 (my life Scripture) begins with that prayer, "You have searched me, Lord, and You know me. You know when I sit and when I rise; You perceive my thoughts from afar…"

Speak to me Your Word. Speak to me Your ways. Please, Father, as Psalm 143:8, "Let the morning bring me word of Your unfailing love, for I have put my trust in You."

I meditate on Your Word, and from my lips escape words from my heart that baffle me: "You have sent me out to the deep."

I sit here in silence.

But You did not abandon me. Though the swells of the sea were mighty and out to swallow me, You—who are faithful if I trust—have kept me by Your grace and have upheld me with Your righteous right hand. "For the Lord's arm is not too short to save." Not even for the one whose life has been thrown into the dark abyss of grief and pain. It is You alone who can save. You alone.

I opened randomly "Streams in the Desert," a classic devotional. After writing the above and as You would orchestrate, the August 30th devotional totally relates to my thoughts, my struggles. It reads, based on Psalm 107:23-24, "They that go down to the sea in ships, that do business in great waters; these see the works of the Lord, and His wonders in the deep." WOW!

The Scripture is divinely meant for me today, speaking and confirming the very revelation You gave me—"You have sent me out to the deep." Is it up to me, Father, whether the swells of the deep swallow me—or keep me from the bashing rocky shore? Is it up to my trust and faith in You?

Could I have been mistaken all along thinking You dropped me in the depths of the sea, abandoned me to arm's length and said, "Swim or perish"? Could it actually have been that I was sent to the deep sea for my own good—my own protection from the enemy who seeks to destroy me on the shore—destroy my testimony—destroy my "purpose"—my story—Your glory in my life?

Could it truly be that You sent me out to the deep so that I would fight hard for my faith and fight hard to keep my eyes out of the swells—and instead on You? Could it be?

Meditate, my soul. Awaken!

Isaiah 30:15

In repentance and rest is your salvation,
   in quietness and trust is your strength.

Calm in the Storm

Meagan E. Ahlstrom

My Jesus is calm in the storm because He is in charge of the storm. While I am stressed, doubtful, or afraid, My Lord is perfectly calm because He is TOTALLY in control. And I serve Him. I know He loves me. So then, should I too not be calm knowing that out of His love for me, He will do what's best for me?

Lord, help me to trust You. I know that is a crazy thing to request because first I have to let go and LEARN to trust You. How can You help me if I can't first do my part by letting go? But Lord, I need help with something bigger— something much bigger. I need Your strength. Not just strength, Lord, but YOUR strength, please.

I am so sad. So hurt. So afraid. Please give me Your strength. I want to be strong for You—for Your will for me. And I want to be strong for me, Lord.

Last year, it was so easy to let go because I genuinely believed there was something better. But then I filled my time with meaningless things—things that aided in my being numb…distant…emotionless. I seemed so together, so strong, so tough, but really I was just closed off and completely unaware of how cold I was. But I have my spirit back! I feel alive again! I am happy. Point is, Lord, I don't want to be that person again. I want to be strong because I AM and not because I have to work at it.

Help me get over this hurt. I couldn't even do my devotional tonight because of it. Forgive me, Lord, please. I need You to heal my heart, although I am not as broken as

I could be. I'm not as broken as I have been in the past. I am stronger than I have been before. I feel it, but I am still hurting. Help me put nothing before You. Even if it is just You and me. Even if for the rest of my life, it is just You and me. I want to honor You. I want to serve You. I want to love You to the best of my ability. I want to give everything else up for You, Lord—for our relationship. May everything else come second.

I know by saying that, I am about to be tested in many ways, challenged and tempted. Lord, keep me strong. Keep me focused. I want to do this for You.

May I pray about everything before acting on it. May I pray about everything instead of believing I have the answers. May I just pray to spend time with You. May I pray knowing that only You, Lord, are in charge of the storm. Calm in the storm because You are totally 100% in charge of the storm. I love You, Lord. Grace. Grace. Please give me Your grace. Let me see what You can do. I love You, Jesus. May I show You all my love for You. Bless You, Lord, for never loving me less. For always making Yourself evident, present—even when I forget.

I cannot shout it out enough! I love You, Lord! You are the ONE true love of my life. May I show You and not just say it!

Amen! Amen! AMEN!

Psalm 73:28

But as for me, it is good to be near God.
  I have made the Sovereign Lord my refuge;
  I will tell of all Your deeds.

Find My Laugh

Rebecca L. Ahlstrom

I could fill a book with ways Meagan challenged me as a person and changed my life forever…

Years ago, Meagan and I were goofing off together in our home in Tennessee, just having some girl time. Meagan, with her unique sense of humor, said something ridiculously funny, and we busted up laughing! She threw her head back and filled the room with that oh-so-contagious Meagan laugh. I, on the other hand, fell to the floor laughing but barely made a sound. In fact, I was laughing with my hands over my mouth. Then, just like that, as though someone muted the TV, she stopped laughing. She looked me square in the eyes and said, "Mom, you need to find your laugh!"

And she was right. She was absolutely right! Why, for so many years, did I suppress my laughter? Why did I not just enjoy the moment, in honest expression—whatever that meant? Was it insecurities? My personality? Could it have been my southern upbringing that made my restrained laugh seem more appealing?

Eventually, I found my laugh. It took a while to overcome the nonsensical inhibitions within, but I did it—I found MY laugh. And, just as important, I remember the day when Meagan noticed my uncovered, unhindered, from-the-soul laugh. No words were needed. Her eyes and that smile said it all! She was proud of ME. She taught me another "life lesson," and it changed me from the inside out.

This summer, when I lost Meagan, laughter left me. In one single second, it was all gone. Her singing. The music. Our laughing. All of it…gone!

I talk to Meagan sometimes when others aren't around. I talk to her, not that she can hear me or in the hope that she will respond, but simply because it warms my soul and soothes my heart.

The other morning when dreams of the crash woke me from a sleep, I chose to focus on Meagan's beautiful smile. Then I could almost hear her laughter. It was at that moment that I felt her in my soul. I remembered her words, those eyes, that smile saying, "Mom, you need to find your laugh." I cried. Then nodded my head. Yes. Yes, I need to find my laugh again…and I will.

Meagan's Misma

Choose One

Rebecca L. Ahlstrom

Meagan reflected for days on what she told me, "Mom, you need to find your laugh!" She just couldn't accept the fact that her mother's laughter was like a silent movie...not when HER laughter was so contagious and amusing. She LOVED to laugh! And it really bothered her that for some crazy reason I could not enjoy this emotion as she did. She seemed to hurt for me.

So...a few nights later, Meagan approached me in our great room. I WILL NEVER FORGET THIS because it was one of her most spectacular performances!! She positioned herself on the floor and said verbatim, "I've been thinking...I'm going to help you find your laugh. I'm going to present a variety of laughs, and you will choose one...until you find your own."

She proceeded to give me at least 20 different options, from a giggle to a boisterous explosion, laughs with different dialects (somehow she made that possible), and my favorite "Dexter's sister" (cartoon). After each, she would pause with a raised eyebrow, and if I didn't latch on, she would continue with another option. Whether planned or unexpected, she had me laughing so hard I was crying. Oh my gosh! I remember this like it was yesterday! Ahhh, Meagan, you are wonderful!! You will ALWAYS be with me!

Psalm 126:2

Our mouths were filled with laughter,
  our tongues with songs of joy.

I Miss You

Meagan E. Ahlstrom

Don't speak.
Just listen to what I have to say.
I love you.
I miss you.
I miss you every day—
All of the time.
I miss your face.
I miss your smile.
I miss your eyes.
I miss the way you look at me.
I miss the way you can read my mind
And see my thoughts.
I miss you.
I miss you because I love you.
And I love the way I miss you.

I'm Proud of Who I Am

Meagan E. Ahlstrom

So, I am a little afraid that one day I will look back at everything I have ever written and think, "Man, there was so much more to me than a boy! Why didn't I ever write about anything else?"

You know, the truth is one day I will be older, more level-headed, and much wiser (if all goes well), and at that time I will see I had so much more to write about. (Granted, I am seeing that now; otherwise, I wouldn't be writing this.)

It's just that I am aware. And I don't ever want there to be a time that I am misinterpreted about being aware! I am aware that the relationships I have and the people I spend time with will help define and shape who I will be. But I am also very aware that there are a hundred other things in my life right now that will do that as well!

I am proud of who I am right now! And I want to document that! I don't do it enough.

And it's NOT because of who I date, but more because of who I am, how I feel, how I think and react to things. It's about what is already in me! And though it might not be the most dramatic or interesting things at times, it is what is inside of me that is really important—an eternal hope from an Almighty God.

A Very Thin Line

Meagan E. Ahlstrom

Lord, I feel I am walking a very thin line. I feel I should pray for my friend now more than ever. At the same time, what I want to pray for is strength in his relationship with You. I know it is always good to pray for strength in your spiritual relationship, but I feel my prayers might come across as judgmental. Lord, forgive me—for that is not my heart. I am a sinner. One who sins every day! I know I have turned my back on You in many ways and at many times. Lord, forgive me for every time I have not honored You in my thoughts and actions, and please know that I want to do better.

I feel for my friend. I feel he knows he does wrong, but it eats him up in a different way. It weighs him down and keeps him from happiness. We are all sinners. We all mess up, but as believers we are forgiven when we ask for forgiveness, and then on top of that, You separate our sins from us as far as the east is from the west! I find such peace in that. I feel I can rest in the knowledge that You love me despite all of my mistakes and flaws. (Lord, please know I am truly sorry.)

All that to say, I know I mess up, and I know I am a work in progress, which is why I feel I can't or shouldn't pray for anyone else's weakness as if I don't have my own. But I care about my friend, Lord. I want him happy and healthy. I want him to see You. And I know prayer is the only sure way I can know he will have those things—which, I suppose, is the only reason I do ultimately feel it is okay to pray for him that way. In fact, I hope I have people in my life always who pray for my relationship and for a deeper connection with You! Always!

Lord, please, be with him. Speak to him. Show him how close You truly are. How real You are—not in the sense that he doubts Your existence, but how "real" You are as in how powerful! How supernatural! May he see that the Christ who lived and walked this earth some 2,000 years ago, who performed miracles and rose from the dead, is the same Christ living within him. Show him, Lord, that it doesn't matter how many books we read or services we attend or trips we take! It's our hearts! It's all about opening up our hearts! Truly believing! Truly believing! Lord, show him who You are! Show me, Lord. Show me! May we never put You in a box! May we never limit what You can do!

Be with my friend, Lord. Help him see and understand where he is and what You are doing. Give him peace, please. May he just be still. May all of his troubled thoughts and all of his worries cease, and may he just rest in You.

I love You, Lord. You have my whole heart!

Amen! Amen! Amen!

Listening

Meagan E. Ahlstrom

"There is no greater loan than a sympathetic ear."
Anonymous

Most of the time, the best thing you can loan someone is a listening, sympathetic ear. Greater is a listening ear than a babbling tongue.

Much of the time, all a person needs is to be heard. Make sure, however, that if someone listens to you, you listen to someone. It could be the same person or someone completely different. But understand that when someone listens to you, they are not only being caring and wonderful; they are also teaching YOU to listen. And know that when you listen to others, whether you realize it or not, YOU are teaching THEM.

An Amazing Time of Self-Discovery

Meagan E. Ahlstrom

It's half past 1am and I can't sleep.

I'm realizing now that so many things have changed, and at first I thought my whole world was over, but I have learned SO much about myself in this time. It has ended up being an amazing time for me—an amazing time of self-discovery. I began to remember all the things I want and love. So many thoughts and feelings were flooding over me. I'm still overwhelmed at times with a million thoughts and feelings even a whole month later.

For the first time in a long time, I am alone and having to fight "life" by myself. That "alone" is such an amazingly weird feeling! Now, I am in the stage of self-awareness. It is remarkable how during such heartbreak, I can also have such a wonderful time in other ways. I am rediscovering myself and my dreams. And I've actually learned so many things about me that I either didn't know or just totally forgot!

What happened to me? When exactly did I lose myself? And where was my head when I let all my friends go? I must have been crazy.

In rediscovering myself, I'm finding I like myself. I'm a good girl and could make someone really happy, and—I think I'm funny. ☺

How could I have spent so much time acting so childish and so darn foolish? I really do want to have a life of my own—a life just of my own.

Lord, what will You do with me?

Maybe When I'm 50

Meagan E. Ahlstrom

How I love to write, and I have written many things—though some of my experiences will die with me, having no evidence of existence.

I don't think of my past much. Sometimes because I am so numb to it, other times because I am so far from it—such as it should be.

I am who I am now despite so much of my past. And, only due to God's saving grace, I will never give power to the darkness meant to destroy me.

So, I won't write about old things. At least not now. Maybe when I'm 50.

[Meagan to herself] Meagan, if you are reading this at 50, it would be nice to know what you think of it all now. I hope I served you and God well.

1 Peter 4:19

So then, those who suffer according to God's will should commit themselves to their faithful Creator and continue to do good.

On the Father's Workbench

Rebecca L. Ahlstrom

I have not found my "new normal" yet, for I am still on the passage of grief. In the early morning hours before the sun comes up, I whisper to God, "Please let this all be a dream." And every morning my heart breaks. When I get up, no words are needed from the heavens. For I just need open my eyes and reality hits me below the belt. Everything has changed. Our home has changed. We are changed. I am broken. And Meagan's things are secretly tucked away in places that are of comfort to me—places I can gently stroke as I walk by, places I can sit and "remember." Everything is different. Her laughter. Her music. Her singing. Her. She is gone.

What remains is the silence of the Master Builder, skillfully and strategically using the pieces of my shattered life to form a unique work of art that will glorify HIM. A work of art being formed with such precision and without the hovering of time. All I can do is listen to my spirit's beckoning to "stay on the Master's workbench, for there I shall see my redemption!" And so every day, I take my heart and lay it at His workshop door...trusting, hoping, believing. It doesn't matter if I am sitting in a corner weeping over my "loss" or caught up in the beauty of my own backyard and oblivious to the world around me. It doesn't matter if I'm in bed, temporarily paralyzed by grief. As long as my heart is on HIS workbench, then HE is at work.

My dad has a fantastic workshop befitting a skilled craftsman, and I love to hear him at work and see the things he has created. Every day, faithfully, I believe he spends time working on something. When I was a little girl, he would give me a few pieces of scrap wood, some nails, and a hammer. I would sit outside his shop and hammer away, pull out the nails and start all over again, and again. It didn't matter what I created; I was near him. That's all I really wanted. So, the sounds, the smells, the time in his workshop even today give me a sense of security with my dad. Seems to be the same with My Father and HIS workshop.

In my quiet time, God has revealed a truth to me: I've had it all wrong. My sentence, "Meagan is gone," is incomplete. Rather, "Meagan has gone ahead!" An answer to my prayers for all my children since they were born...that HE would keep them, protect them, save them, etc., and that they would see Him face to face one glorious day. I forgot in all those years that HE chooses the day, not me. I was not prepared. OH, BUT Meagan was!

Today, I feel the chiseling, the stroke of HIS hammer, the fire. It doesn't matter that I see the shattered pieces of my life strewn around. By HIS grace and for HIS glory, someday HE will reveal a more beautiful, more radiant, and more resilient work of art. As long as I continue to surrender my heart to His workshop door, then I am in good hands. I am in the BEST HANDS. The hands of THE MASTER BUILDER, MY CREATOR.

Isaiah 41:10

So do not fear, for I am with you,
   do not be dismayed, for I am your God.
I will strengthen you and help you;
   I will uphold you with My righteous right hand.

Come Home to Me

Meagan E. Ahlstrom

Listen!
Now that I've got you sitting still.
I am Lord God.
I am Jesus Christ.
I am your Father, child.
I cry with you when I see your tears
And all of your pain.
I've felt it too.

Come home to Me.
Come home to Me.
Don't you know I'm waiting for you?
Come home to Me.
Come home to Me,
To all I am and all I have for you.
Come home to Me,
Home to a love that is true.

He wasn't talking about my pain from my illness. He was referring to the pain I had suffered over the last three or four years without Him or away from Him. My illness was just His way to get me to sit down! And LISTEN!

I made a choice to ask Him into my heart, and that is where He lives. I asked Him then to take control, and I feel He tried nicer ways but ultimately had to be more drastic to get me to chill.

He has plans for me, for this life I've asked Him to lead. And if I lose sight, He will help me get refocused…by any means necessary!

He lives in my heart, and I asked Him to take control a long time ago. And as always…He is FAITHFUL!

A Geek of Writing

Meagan E. Ahlstrom

I feel that when it comes to writing, I am somewhat of a geek. Although I have many known weaknesses, my love for writing seems to outweigh my insecurities.

I took an AP English class in high school that focused on writing essays. We would spend the whole class period writing any thoughts or ideas that we had about plays we read, political issues, or simply about ourselves. I also keep a journal, write poems, and relieve tension through writing. It is definitely a passion of mine!

I keep anywhere between three to five different journals at any given time. I have a journal where I write love letters to the Lord. A journal about mundane events that may occur on an average day. I have a journal for each guy that I have seriously dated. These journals I begin months after the breakup when I feel I have the best perspective. I write these journals as if my young daughters, that hopefully God will allow me to have some day, will read them. I also keep a journal about deep thoughts, political views, or my standards on certain issues.

I love to write. I feel it is a way of relaxation. I have two jobs, one where I sit for long periods of time doing nothing. On those days I access the office computer and type for hours. I type about anything that comes to mind. And I usually end up with pages and pages of whatever it was I was thinking.

I write poetry and sometimes transform the poems into songs. I will read a book and then write about similar experiences I related to in the story in the same technique and tone the author used. I have notebooks beyond notebooks, loose pages beyond loose pages of writings. I am constantly writing.

Although I write on a regular basis, I feel having been out of school for a while has harmed me. I am out of practice when it comes to my grammar and mechanic usage. I get lost when trying to determine just where to put those darn commas. And when it comes to a thesis statement, I might as well wave a white flag.

I write from my heart, my mind, the core of me. And although it is a very relaxing and enjoyable task, I do not have the skills to write like a professional. I feel that through my writings I portray my intellect in many, many ways. One day, I hope I can be seen as an intelligent, professional writer, as well as an imaginative, passionate one!

One day.

Philippians 1:20-21

So I eagerly expect and hope that I will in no way be ashamed, but will have sufficient courage so that now as always Christ will be exalted in my body, whether by life or by death. For to me, to live is Christ and to die is gain.

The Train Ride

Rebecca L. Ahlstrom

What I can say now I could not have said right after the tragedy. I could not have said it even a couple of years ago.

The other day I had a vision while I was sitting in the quiet of my home—my journey is like a train ride! Our tragedy threw me on a tumultuous train that seemed out of control. Sometimes it moved so fast I was thrown from side to side and could not catch my breath; traveling in no obvious direction except "crazy forward"; everything a blur—all I could do was cry "Jesus!"; the train taking the turns so hard the screeching of the wheels drowns out everything but my pain; often flipping upside down where nothing makes sense and I can't find my place; going up and down, turning and jerking; over creaky narrow bridges sure to crumble beneath me; through dark, seemingly endless tunnels to break forth into blinding sunshine, only to enter yet another tunnel longer than the last; other times moving so eerily slowly that grief shackles my feet from being able to do anything good and right for Your name's sake.

Though the train is violent and unpredictable, I don't get off! I don't dare get off! I hang on for my life. I hang on for my faith. I hang on for my family. After all, "where could I go that You would not find me!" Psalm 139 quickly became my "Life Scripture."

I am in a desperate situation. No one around me can see the train I am on. No one can understand the raging storms within me of grief, guilt, anger, confusion, abandonment, doubt...rivaling with my faith, clinging to my One hope and my relationship with my personal Savior, my commitment to You, Your commitment to me, Your Word. I shut people out and have pursued You for my sanity! And when I have been so exhausted, and could not hang on and stay on the reckless train any longer, YOU HELD ON TO ME! YOU didn't let go.

You proved Your Word time and time again, "In my weakness, Your strength is revealed." And nothing, "no one can snatch me out of my Father's hand!"

I stay on the train. I can't get off and just exist. Some get off and try to bury the cross they were meant to bear, simply going through the motions of life. I don't want to be one of those people. Just "existing" would not glorify You, my Father, nor would it honor my daughter. We are called to be "salt of the earth," and when we go through a personal hell, I think we should become at some point...well...even saltier!

No! I'm going to hang on and continue to pursue You, Jesus, with tenacity. I want to get so close to You that I start to look like You! The Bible is filled with many verses that continue to save me, one being, "Run the race in order that you may win the prize." Run the race in order that you may win the prize! And what is the prize? My husband shared his revelation years ago that rose up in me while on this journey, "We've been taught by so many that the prize is a crown of jewels when we die; or it's a place in heaven; or it's my own mansion on the streets of gold. But to me at the end of the race, the prize is to look more like Jesus, my Savior."

Lord, You brought that revelation alive to my soul during one of the darkest tunnels. In the end, we will all stand before God for the things we have done, and I believe that You will be by my side as my advocate. I fall way short of the hope of hearing God say, "Well done, my good and faithful servant." What keeps me going is not a "works" mentality but a "purpose" mentality. Oh, God forbid that I should hear, "Oh, Rebecca, I had so much for you to do." Rather, I would hope for a simple, "You tried, Rebecca." Then God will notice my scars like His Son's from the lashes of life and the cross we had to bear, and He will smile.

Though I am dashed against the rocks at times, and fires singe my skin; though my heart aches intensely for my Meagan, I am going to hold fast by Your grace. And in those moments when my weakness causes me to lose my grip, YOU will yet again prove Yourself to me…YOU WILL NEVER LET GO! And at random points on that crazy, almost unbearable train ride, I look to the window and catch a glimpse of my reflection—THE REFLECTION of You holding me—and I am reminded, You are with me…I am NOT alone. I will make it, because You have me. And though I can't see the train conductor, You will give me the assurance that it is You all the while! And You will help me glory in the cross by Your mercy and inexhaustible grace! I am in my defining moment!

Reader Reflections

"This is unbelievable! And so 'Meagan'. I loved the way her brain worked. It inspires me." ~ Julie Salzmann

"In everything I read from her, she seems so satisfied in Christ, so content with Him, and so trusting of where He had her in life." ~ Carla Kopp

"God is still speaking and teaching us thru Meag's writings...she truly lives on still in this earth, teaching and encouraging us. The wisdom she penned could only come from her Creator...so we know these words have life-changing power. They are living words." ~ Luis Ramirez

"Rebecca, Just a beautiful window into the journey God is on with you. I'm so grateful for your transparency. Much like Meagan's, it is challenging and convicting all those who cross your path to walk more intimately, love more deeply and surrender more completely to Jesus." ~ Kaye Price Downey

"Meagan's writing is gifted, inspired and relevant! I have been amazed at her maturity and insight for one so young. Thank you so much for sharing her intimate thoughts with us...we are blessed!" ~ Jo Roetman

"When I first met her at Lauder in Cool Springs she said to me, 'I feel so lucky to be your friend. I feel like everyone wants to be in your group and I'm one of the chosen ones.' It always made me laugh because what she didn't realize was that everyone wanted to be HER friend. I felt so blessed to even know Meagan. She always put others first and I don't think she could even fathom how much she was loved and admired by everyone she met. She was truly an angel." ~ Brandon Reece

"After reading your post this is all I can say with tears pouring down my face…this morning…this is how my Father God chose to speak to me this morning…through your post which is actually a peek into Meagan's life and relationship with her Father God. Wow…how long…how many times will God teach me through Meagan Ahlstrom's life…a girl I didn't even know?" ~ Jan Schexnayder

"It was evident in Meagan's life, and now through her writings, that she knew a relationship with Christ is something that is not just once attained but needs continual work. A relationship with Jesus is something that takes time and effort, has ebbs and flows, and is something that can change us. When we are honest about our questions, struggles and joys, God can use our journey to inspire the people around us…and even around the world. That is what Meagan was all about, living an authentic life for Jesus out loud and inviting all the world be a part of her amazing journey. I'm thrilled to see how God continues to use her writings to inspire others to do the same." ~ Sara Emmerson

"Wow! God's timing is amazing again, those words could've been pulled from my head and heart, not written as eloquently but with that same thought. I am so sorry God, You are my everything!!" ~ Michelle Parent-Shambora

"I tell everyone about her…. She lives on in the hearts of everyone that knew her! To know her was to love her!!!! Even those that never met her have been blessed by her journals. Thank you for sharing Meagan with the world." ~ Lisa Tice

"I misssssssssss it sooooo badly! What a light she was in my life! …she is stunning and that was just so her, I mean just so stunning!!! Then she was just this beautiful soul on the inside, it was like is this girl real! Loved my time with her! We laughed a lot! Talked and got each other cards and held each other up in a very awkward time in both of our lives. The laughs though were usually the kind where you had to hold your side! Will never, never forget my Meagan!" ~ Jessie Meeks

"I don't believe in past lives, but if I did, I would have sworn that Meagan and I had known each other in another life. We were instant friends the night we met through a mutual friend in Franklin, Tennessee. Her faith and family were the oxygen that fed the fire that was Meagan. I count myself a very blessed man to have crossed paths with this beautiful soul. A few days before the tragedy, she texted me and asked if we could have a 'phone date' sometime over the weekend. We hadn't had one of our talks in way too long, and I was over the moon to catch up with my dear friend. However, the weekend came and went with no call from Meagan. I watched my phone all weekend to no avail. It wasn't until Monday that I found out the earth shattering reason why. Meagan, I look forward to 'a streets of gold' date with you one day. Thank you for being you. Thank you, God, for sharing her with me for a little while." ~ Shannon Bain

"Meagan introduced me to journaling or speaking to God through writing letters to Him when we were roommates. She inspired me to start journaling one day when I was going through a difficult time in my life. She thought it was so important that I started this new way of speaking to God that she bought me my first journal — one terribly over-priced journal that I turned down buying for myself when I saw the price. And as we walked out the doors of [the bookstore], she turns and says, 'Here you go!' No excuse. I had to journal. Meagan freely gave from her heart. Never missed a beat in letting her LIGHT shine. I will cherish my friendship with her and the impact of knowing her changed me. I am forever grateful to God for putting Meagan in my life. Without that friendship, I would have never been able to 'lay it all out there on paper to Him.' And she continues to change me through her journal entries." ~ Ashley Tyrell

"I'm silently letting your words fill my soul. Amen. XOXO" ~ Beckie Untiedt

"This is our God! He is still redeeming…life out of death…. His story lives on through one of His faithful servants…and her advocates." ~ Laurie A. Mueller

"Wow! What a blessing to know her faith is now sight!" ~ Leah Fort

"I love how Meagan talks to Jesus. She's there. She had a revelation. I can only imagine the closeness and joy she felt with Him in those moments. WOW!" ~ Kimi Zwart

Meagan E. Ahlstrom, voted "Most Likely to Succeed," was a college student studying six languages, was an English tutor to the Hispanic community, and used her gift as a make-up artist to inspire her clients. She was involved in theatre, an avid writer, and passionate about singing, and she loved animals. Most importantly, Meagan wanted, in her own words, "to live an extraordinary life that could never have been accomplished without the favor and grace of God...A life that will make a difference...The only thing that will matter is that I lived a life loving the Lord and my family and those close to me...And I am certain I have loved with my whole heart."

Rebecca L. Ahlstrom speaks in a wide variety of environments, from churches to high schools, and as a voice for Mothers Against Drunk Driving (MADD). She has been an avid journaler all her life and has taught writing workshops in the States and abroad. She currently resides in the Nashville, Tennessee, area with her husband, Leonard, who is a worship pastor, songwriter and producer. Together they have three children, three grandchildren, and a Rhodesian Ridgeback named Beaux.

For more, visit www.facebook.com/groups/MeaganAhlstrom

www.rebeccaahlstrom.com

Meagan